Diana Shermeyer

By Diana Shermeyer

Chez Diana

A COLLECTION OF FAVORITE RECIPES

Cover and Graphic Design by
Mindy Kuhn, President of Blue Butterfly Creative
www.blue-butterfly-creative.com

Blue Butterfly Creative
pr · marketing · design

Second printing 2012.
ISBN: 978-0-615-60072-7
Printed by Lehigh Phoenix

Author's Note: Some of these recipes are my
family recipes and others are compiled from
different sources. The recipes from other sources
are shown as they originally appeared.

Table of Contents

Appetizers

Chez Diana

Crab Mold

From Southern Living 1985 Annual Recipes
Page 318

Ingredients

2 envelopes unflavored gelatin
½ cup cold water
½ cup boiling water
3 (8-ounce) packages cream cheese, soft
¾ cup lemon juice
1 teaspoon salt
1 teaspoon Worcestershire sauce
½ teaspoon hot sauce
½ teaspoon grated onion
4 (6-ounce) cans lump crabmeat, drained
Pimiento-stuffed olive slices
Chopped fresh parsley

Directions

Sprinkle gelatin over cold water; let stand five minutes.
Add boiling water; stir until gelatin dissolves.
Combine gelatin mixture, cream cheese, lemon juice, salt, Worcestershire sauce, hot sauce, and onion in a mixing bowl; beat at medium speed with an electric mixer until smooth. Stir in crabmeat; pour into a lightly oiled 5 ½ cup mold, and chill until firm.
Unmold and garnish with olives and parsley.
Serve with crackers.

Yield: 5 ½ cups

Sausage Treats

from Tina Bazley

Ingredients

1 pound hot sausage
1 ½ pound sharp cheddar cheese
3 cups Bisquick

Directions

Mix ingredients together. Make little balls and place on a greased baking pan. Bake for 12-15 minutes at 400 degrees.

Spinach Artichoke Dip

Ingredients

1 package (10 ounces) frozen chopped Spinach
½ cup artichoke hearts drained
3 scallions chopped
2 cloves garlic
1 ½ cups plain low fat yogurt
3 Tbsp. parmesan cheese
2 Tbsp. reduced fat cream cheese

Place all ingredients in blender. Blend on high speed until smooth. Refrigerate three hours before serving. Serve with crackers or raw vegetables.

Makes 8 servings

Clam Dip
(Pictured above)

Ingredients

¼ lb. butter
2 cans minced clams
1 Tbsp. lemon juice
½ green pepper chopped
1 onion chopped fine
¼ cup bread crumbs
1 tsp. Tabasco
1 tsp. oregano
1 tsp. parsley
Parmesan cheese

Cook first 5 ingredients in small pan and simmer 15 minutes. Add all the ingredients to the clam mixture and put in a small casserole dish. Sprinkle top with Parmesan cheese. Bake for 30 minutes at 350 degrees. Serve with crackers.

Chez Diana

Seven-Layer Mexican Dip

You'll be the hit of the party with this crowd-pleasing dip. We lightened it up with low-fat cheese, fat-free bean dip and sour cream — nobody will notice the difference. Serve with Tostitos or scoops.

Ingredients

1 cup fat-free sour cream
2 Tbsp reduced-sodium taco seasoning
9 oz fat-free bean dip, about 1 heaping cup
6 oz guacamole, about ¾ cup
¼ cup low-fat shredded cheddar cheese
4 medium scallions, chopped
1 small tomato, chopped
6 medium olives, black, sliced

Directions

Combine sour cream and taco seasoning; mix well. Spread bean dip on bottom of a 12-inch round glass serving bowl or edged-platter. Top with guacamole, sour cream, cheese, scallions, tomatoes and olives.

Yields about ¼ cup dip per serving.

The World's Best Guacamole Recipe

Source: Wild Oats Natural Marketplace

Ingredients

3 ripe organic avocados, peeled and pitted
juice of 1 lime
1 medium ripe tomato, diced (optional)
¼ cup fresh cilantro, finely chopped
¼ cup red onion, finely chopped
½ teaspoon minced garlic
4 dashes Texas Champagne Cayenne Pepper Sauce
½ teaspoon ground cumin
½ teaspoon sugar
salt to taste
parsley, chopped fine (optional for garnish)

Serves 2 to 4

Directions

Mash the avocados in a bowl with a fork until slightly lumpy. Stir in the lime juice, tomato, cilantro, red onion and garlic. Add the Tabasco (use extra if you like spicy), cumin, salt and sugar. Mix well. Sample and add more seasonings if desired.

Cover the bowl and chill or let stand at room temperature for one hour to allow the flavors to blend. Serve as you like it!

Chez Diana

Spinach with Chickpeas

Source: © Eating Well Magazine

Enjoy this vegetable-rich nibble as they do in Spain,
spooned onto small rounds of fresh or lightly toasted bread.

Make Ahead Tip: Cover and refrigerate for up to 2 days.
Bring to room temperature or reheat on medium-low heat before serving.

Ingredients

2 pounds baby spinach
3 tablespoons extra-virgin olive oil, divided
1 medium red onion, finely chopped
5 cloves garlic, minced
1 19-ounce can chickpeas, rinsed
1 ½ teaspoons dried thyme
1 ½ teaspoons dried oregano
1 ½ teaspoons ground cumin
1 teaspoon kosher salt
½ teaspoon hot paprika
½ cup golden raisins
½ cup reduced-sodium chicken broth or vegetable broth

12 servings, about ½ cup each

Directions

Rinse spinach and let drain in a colander. With water still
clinging to it, place half the spinach in a Dutch oven over
medium heat. Cook, tossing with tongs and adding the
remaining spinach by the handful until all is added and
wilted, 6 to 8 minutes. Drain in the colander.
Let cool slightly, then coarsely chop.

Carefully wipe out the pan, then heat 1 tablespoon oil over
medium heat. Add onion and garlic and cook, stirring, until
the onion is tender and lightly browned, 8 to 10 minutes. Stir in
chickpeas, thyme, oregano, cumin, salt and paprika. Using
a potato masher, mash some of the chickpeas, then cook, stirring,
for 3 minutes. Stir in raisins and broth, scraping up any browned
bits. Add the chopped spinach and stir gently to combine. Remove
from the heat and let stand 10 minutes. Drizzle with the remaining
2 tablespoons oil just before serving.

Easy Cheese Log

Easy and Delicious

Ingredients

Equal parts: Feta, crumbled Havarti, shredded Cream cheese
Green onion, diced
Slivered almonds, ground

Directions

Chill, or freeze, Havarti in order to grate if you don't use pre-grated.
Add Feta and Cream cheese and minced green onion and microwave
for 1 minute on very low power to soften. Mix thoroughly and shape
into a ball or a log. Roll in chopped slivered almonds. Wrap in plastic
and chill to firm

Onion Pie — Germany

Recipes on Parade Foreign Foods
Mrs. Andrew J. Colyer, Pres. Walter Reed Army Medical Center
Washington, DC

Ingredients

1 pizza pastry (I use frozen pie crust)
2 or 3 medium onions, finely chopped
2 to 3 Tbsp. butter or margarine
½ tsp. cumin
½ tsp. salt
Dash of pepper
6 slices of bacon, crisply fried and crumbled
1 egg yolk, beaten
¾ cup sour cream

Directions

Preheat oven to 400 degrees. Cook onions in butter until clear, not
brown; cool. Spread on pastry; sprinkle with cumin, salt, pepper and
bacon. Bake for about 20 minutes; remove from oven. Fold egg yolk
into sour cream; pour over pastry. Return to oven; bake for 10 to 15
minutes or until golden brown. Cool; slice in small wedges and serve as
an appetizer.

Yield: 12-14 servings

Chez Diana

Deviled Ham & Cheese Spread

Great for parties with Ritz crackers!

Ingredients

1 can (4 ¼ ounces) deviled ham (spread)
1 cup cheddar cheese (shredded)
3 oz. cream cheese (softened)
3 Tbsp. chilies (chopped green)
2 Tbsp. green onions (finely chopped)
Ritz crackers

Directions

BEAT all ingredients except crackers in small bowl with electric mixer on medium speed until well blended; cover. REFRIGERATE at least 1 hour or until chilled. SERVE as a spread with crackers.

Serves 12

Southwestern Layered Bean Dip

This classic party dip is made with lower-fat sour cream, plenty of fiber-rich beans and vegetables; and it's still just as delicious. Scoop it up with tortilla chips.

Ingredients

1 16-ounce can fat-free refried beans, preferably spicy
1 15-ounce can black beans, rinsed
4 scallions, sliced
½ cup prepared salsa
½ teaspoon ground cumin
½ teaspoon chili powder
¼ cup pickled jalapeno slices, chopped
1 cup shredded Monterey Jack or Cheddar cheese
½ cup reduced-fat sour cream
1 ½ cups, chopped romaine lettuce
1 medium tomato, chopped
1 medium avocado, chopped
¼ cup canned sliced black olives, (optional)

Directions

Combine refried beans, black beans, scallions, salsa, cumin, chili powder and jalapenos in a medium bowl. Transfer to a shallow 2-quart microwave-safe dish; sprinkle with cheese.

Microwave on High until the cheese is melted and the beans are hot, 3 to 5 minutes.

Spread sour cream evenly over the hot bean mixture, then scatter with lettuce, tomato, avocado and olives (if using).

12 Servings   Prep: 20 minutes

Chez Diana

Jojo's Black Bean & Corn Dip

Healthy Serving

Ingredients

1 (14.5 oz.) can black beans, rinsed & drained
1 can or frozen whole kernel corn, drained & cooked
1 medium red onion, chopped
1 red bell pepper, chopped
1 jalapeno pepper, chopped
2 tbsp. fresh cilantro, chopped
2 tbsp. freshly squeezed lemon juice
1 tbsp. olive oil
¼ tsp. salt

Directions

Combine all ingredients and mix well.
Serve at room temperature with tortilla chips, or as a side dish. Enjoy!

Quick Hummus

1995 Southern Living Cookbook – Page 93

Ingredients

1 or 2 cloves garlic
1 (15-ounce) can garbanzo beans, drained
¼ cup tahini
2 tablespoons lemon juice
2 tablespoons water
¼ tsp. salt

Directions

Pulse garlic in food processor until chopped. Add garbanzo beans and remaining ingredients; process until smooth. Serve with pita bread or assorted raw vegetables.

Yield: 1 ½ cups

Oven Chicken Fingers

Oven Chicken Fingers are tender, golden strips of breaded chicken with a tempting sauce for dipping. The recipe comes from Mary Peterson of Charlestown, Rhode Island.

Ingredients

1 cup Italian bread crumbs
2 tablespoons grated
  Parmesan cheese
1 garlic clove, minced
¼ cup vegetable oil
6 boneless, skinless chicken
  breast halves

Honey Mustard Sauce

2 tablespoons cornstarch
1 cup water, divided
½ cup honey
¼ cup prepared mustard

Directions

In a plastic bag, mix bread crumbs and Parmesan cheese; set aside. In a small bowl, combine garlic and oil. Flatten the chicken to ½-in. thickness; cut into 1- in. - wide strips. Dip strips in oil; coat with crumb mixture. Place on a greased baking sheet. Bake at 350 degrees for 20 minutes or until golden brown. For honey mustard sauce, dissolve cornstarch in 1 tablespoon water in a saucepan. Add honey, mustard and remaining water; bring to a boil over medium heat. Boil for 1 minute, stirring constantly. Serve with chicken for dipping.

Tuna Mold

Looks and Tastes Like Salmon!
From The Rainbow Cooks Soups, Salads & Specialties – Page 50
Serves 6

3 (7 ½ oz.) cans tuna
1 cup chopped celery
½ cup chopped onion
1 cup mayonnaise
1 (8 oz.) package cream cheese, softened
1 envelope gelatin
½ cup cold water
1 can tomato soup

Drain and flake tuna. Heat tomato soup and add cream cheese, stirring with a wire whisk until smooth. Sprinkle gelatin on cold water to dissolve. Stir gelatin into soup. Blend in mayonnaise and then add tuna, celery and onion. Pour into oiled 4 cup mold. Chill overnight. Unmold and garnish with stuffed green olives, tomatoes or cucumber slices.

NOTE: You may use salmon or crabmeat in lieu of tuna. I serve with Ritz crackers or triscuits.

Buffalo Chicken Fingers

These garlic-and-cayenne-soaked chicken breast morsels are baked instead of fried for a low fat version of Buffalo Wings
Servings: 8

Ingredients

4 skinless, boneless chicken breast halves —cut into finger-sized pieces
¼ cup all-purpose flour
1 teaspoon garlic powder
1 teaspoon cayenne pepper
½ teaspoon salt
¾ cup bread crumbs
2 egg whites, beaten
1 tablespoon water

Directions

Preheat oven to 400 degrees F (205 degrees C). Coat a baking sheet with a nonstick spray. In a bag, mix together flour, ½ teaspoon garlic powder, ½ teaspoon cayenne pepper, and 1/4 teaspoon salt. On a plate, mix the bread crumbs with the rest of the garlic powder, cayenne pepper, and salt. Shake the chicken pieces with the seasoned flour. Beat egg whites with 1 tablespoon water, and place egg mixture in a shallow dish or bowl. Dip seasoned chicken in egg mixture, then roll in the seasoned bread crumb mixture. Place on prepared baking sheet. Bake for about 8 minutes in the preheated oven. Use tongs to turn pieces over. Bake 8 minutes longer, or until chicken juices run clear.

Soups—Chilled & Hot

Chez Diana

Avocado Banana Chilled Soup

A chilled soup. Great for summer. By *Parsley*

Ingredients

2 ripe Hass avocados, peeled, pitted and diced
2 large ripe bananas, peeled and sliced
1 cup milk
¾-1 cup sugar (start low)
4 tablespoons lemon juice
½ teaspoon cinnamon
⅛ teaspoon nutmeg
1 quart plain yogurt
salt, if needed, to taste (I don't use any)

Directions

1. In a blender or food processor, puree avocados and bananas.
2. Add the milk, sugar, lemon juice, cinnamon, nutmeg and yogurt; blend until smooth.
3. Add salt, if needed.
4. Chill at least 3 hours prior to serving.

Chilled Banana Soup

Exported from MasterCook

Ingredients

2 tablespoons butter
1 large onion — finely chopped
2 cups chicken stock
¾ cup shredded unsweetened coconut
2 ripe bananas — in 1" pieces
3 ½ cups milk
6 small sprigs mint

Serving Size: 6

Directions

1. Melt the butter in a 4-quart soup pot. Add the chopped onion and cover with a piece of wax paper, and steam on low heat until the onion is transparent. Remove the wax paper. Add the stock and coconut and bring to a boil.
2. Place the banana pieces in a blender and puree them, gradually pouring in the soup mixture. Blend until smooth.
3. Return the mixture to the pot and stir in the milk. Lower heat and simmer for 5 minutes.

Chill and serve cold. Garnish each serving with a small mint sprig

Chez Diana

Banana Vichyssoise Soup

Exported from MasterCook

Ingredients

1 cup diced raw potato
½ cup diced onion
1 cup diced peeled apple
½ cup sliced celery
1 banana peeled & sliced
1 ½ cups chicken broth — well
   seasoned
½ teaspoon salt
1 tablespoon butter
½ teaspoon curry
1 cup heavy cream

Directions

Put potato, apple, celery, banana, onion & broth into a saucepan. Cover, bring to a boil.

Simmer over low heat until tender, about 15 min. Put in blender; add salt, butter & curry powder.

Cover & blend until smooth, about 30 seconds. Stir in cream and chill thoroughly.

Serve garnished with chives.

Makes 4 cups

Veronica's Blueberry and Banana Soup

Great for a hot summer's day. 2¼ hours | 15 min prep | SERVES 6

Ingredients

4 bananas
3 tablespoons lemon juice
6 cups apple juice
¼ cup sugar
1 ½ tablespoons cornstarch
½ teaspoon cinnamon
2 ½ cups heavy
   cream
2 cups
blueberries

Recipe Directions

In a food processor (or use a hand held blender), puree bananas with lemon juice. Place in a pot and bring to a boil with 3-½ cups apple juice. Add the sugar; set aside. Blend the cornstarch into the remaining 2-½ cups of apple juice. Add to the soup; simmer for 2 minutes. Remove and chill. Add the cinnamon to the cream. Whip into the soup. Stir in the blueberries. Serve into chilled soup bowls.

Chilled Blueberry Soup

My granddaughter Siena loves this soup.
Serves 4

Ingredients
2 pints blueberries
1 ²/₃ cups water
½ cup honey
1 cup plain yogurt
Pinch of cinnamon

Recipe Directions
In a medium saucepan combine the berries, water and honey. Heat to gentle simmer and cook 20 minutes. Puree mixture in a blender. Transfer to serving bowl and stir in the yogurt. Season with cinnamon. Cover and refrigerate at least 3 hours. Serve.

Zucchini and Dill Soup

Ingredients
2 oz. butter
1 onion, peeled and chopped
6 zucchinis sliced
2 potatoes, peeled and diced
1 ¾ pints water or stock
Salt and pepper to taste
2 Tbsp. chopped dill

Recipe Directions
Melt butter in large pan and sweat the onion until soft. Add potatoes and soften. Add zucchinis and season with salt & pepper. Add stock and bring to a boil. Cook rapidly for 5-10 minutes until the potatoes are tender. Puree. Add the dill. Cover and chill.
Serves 4.

Chez Diana

Cold Buttermilk Raspberry Soup

Ingredients

½ pint fresh raspberries
1 quart buttermilk
$^1/_3$ cup sugar
2 egg yolks
1 teaspoon lemon cream
1 cup heavy cream

Serves 4

Directions

Reserve 4 berries for garnish. Pour remaining berries into bowl. With a fork gently mash the berries to release some juices. Stir in buttermilk, sugar, egg yolks, and lemon juice. Whip cream. Reserve half for garnish and fold remaining whipped cream into soup. To serve, float a dollop of whipped cream & place a raspberry on each dollop.

Banana Soup – Cold

35 minutes total
5 minutes preparation

Ingredients

2 cups milk
½ cup heavy cream
2 large ripe bananas
¼ teaspoon nutmeg
½ tablespoon lemon juice

Directions

Combine all ingredients in a blender and process until very smooth. Chill in the refrigerator for about ½ hour. Serve in chilled bowls and enjoy. Garnish with fresh mint leaves.

Serves 2

Cantaloupe Soup

Ingredients
1 Cantaloupe, cut in chunks
1 cup plain yogurt
¾ cup orange juice
1 Tbsp. honey
¼ tsp. nutmeg
¼ tsp. salt
Pinch of cayenne
Mint leaves for garnish

Directions
Put half of the cantaloupe in a blender with the yogurt and blend until smooth. Add the remaining cantaloupe and blend until smooth. Pour into a large bowl. Add the orange juice, honey, nutmeg, salt, and cayenne and blend until well mixed.

Chill at least one hour before serving. Garnish with mint sprigs to serve.

Serves 8

Minted Cantaloupe Soup

Ingredients
1 Cantaloupe, cut in chunks
1 Tbsp. lime juice
2 Tbsp. honey
1 cup water
½ cup mint or basil leaves

Directions
In a small saucepan, over medium heat, combine sugar, honey, lime juice and water. Cook, stirring until sugar is dissolved. Bring to simmer. Add mint and simmer for 1 minute. Remove from heat, set aside to steep until cooled to room temperature. Place cantaloupe in a glass bowl and strain the syrup over the cantaloupe discarding the mint leaves. Stir to coat cantaloupe. Infuse for 20 minutes. Blend/puree until smooth. Cover and refrigerate until chilled through, about 2 hours before serving.

Serves 6

Chez Diana

Peach-Yogurt Soup

This refreshing, cool soup works as a first-course or a dessert.
Presented by: Better Homes and Gardens ®

Ingredients

2 cups peeled peaches or frozen unsweetened peach slices
¾ cup peach or apricot nectar
1 ½ teaspoon lemon juice
¼ teaspoon ground cinnamon
1 8-ounce carton vanilla yogurt

Prep time: 20 minutes
Makes 4 side-dish servings.

Directions

1. Thaw peaches, if frozen. Do not drain. Place peach slices, peach or apricot nectar, lemon juice, and cinnamon in a blender or food processor bowl. Cover and blend or process until smooth.
2. If desired, reserve 2 tablespoons of the yogurt for garnish. In a large mixing bowl stir a little of the peach mixture into the remaining yogurt, stirring until smooth. Stir in the remaining peach mixture.
3. Cover and chill for 2 to 24 hours. If desired, garnish with the reserved yogurt, mint sprigs, and raspberries.

Chilled Asparagus Soup

Yield: Makes about 1 ½ quarts; 6 servings

Ingredients

1 tablespoon olive oil
1 onion (about 8 oz.), peeled and chopped
2 pounds asparagus, rinsed, tough stem ends snapped off, cut into 2-inch lengths
About 2 ½ cups fat-skimmed chicken broth or vegetable broth
1 cup whipping cream
Salt and pepper

Directions

Pour olive oil into a 3- to 4-quart pan over medium-high heat. When hot, add onion and stir often until limp, 4 to 5 minutes. Add asparagus and 2 ½ cups broth. Bring to a boil over high heat, and then reduce heat and simmer, stirring occasionally, until asparagus is very tender when pierced, 10 to 14 minutes. Working in batches and holding lid down with a towel, whirl asparagus mixture in a blender until very smooth. Pour into a large bowl and stir in cream. Add salt and pepper to taste. Cover and chill until cold, at least 2 hours. If soup is too thick, stir in a little more broth. Taste, and add more salt and pepper if desired. Ladle soup into 6 wide, shallow bowls.

Curried Cold Pea Soup

(Pictured below)
4 servings

Ingredients

10 ½ oz. chicken broth
10 oz. package frozen peas
1 Tbsp. chopped onion
1 tsp. curry powder
1 tsp. lemon juice
¼ tsp. pepper
½ cup yogurt

Directions

Bring broth to a boil. Add peas and simmer for 10 minutes.

Add all but yogurt and puree or blend. Stir in the yogurt and chill.

Serve with a dollop of yogurt.

Chez Diana

Curried Pea Soup

From The Rainbow Cooks Soups, Salads & Specialties Cookbook

Ingredients

1 cup shelled fresh peas
1 small carrot
1 stalk celery with leaves, chopped
1 medium potato
1 medium onion, chopped
1 tsp. salt
1 clove garlic
1 tsp. curry powder
2 cups chicken stock
¾ cups heavy cream

Place vegetables, seasonings and 1 cup of stock in pan and bring to a boil. Cover, reduce heat, and simmer 15 minutes.
Transfer soup to a blender and puree at high speed. Pour remaining 1 cup of stock and ½ cup of the heavy cream. Continue to blend until very smooth. Chill thoroughly.
Whip the remaining heavy cream and use as garnish just before serving.

Serves 6

Chilled Avocado Soup

From The Rainbow Cooks Soups, Salads & Specialties Cookbook
Rich, but Good!

Ingredients

2 ripe avocados
1 13 oz. can of chicken broth
6 Tbsp. sour cream
½ cup half and half
¼ cup lemon juice
½ tsp. salt
Finely chopped onion
Thin slices of lemon
Chopped cilantro

Serves 4

Peel avocados and dice coarsely. Put in blender with broth, sour cream, half and half, lemon juice, salt and chopped onion to taste. Blend until pureed.
Chill thoroughly. Serve in chilled bowls with a garnish of sliced lemon and chopped cilantro.

Note: If desired, 2 Tbsp. of sherry may be added.

Chez Diana

Chilled Corn Soup

This summer soup is pure essence of corn. Blanching the basil, an herb that tends to blacken once it's cut, keeps it jewel green. From Sunset Magazine.

Ingredients
9 medium-size ears fresh
  yellow corn
½ cup fresh basil leaves
salt
¼ cup extra-virgin olive oil

Yield: Makes about 6 cups

Boil corn in salted water, covered, 2 to 3 minutes. (For a smoky flavor, you can also roast or grill the ears instead of boiling them.) Slice kernels off the ears with a sharp paring knife. In two batches, purée kernels in a blender with 4 cups water. Strain purée into a bowl, pressing to squeeze out the corn liquid, and throw away the kernel mash. Add salt to taste and chill soup until cold, at least 3 hours. Meanwhile, boil tightly packed fresh basil leaves for 2 to 3 seconds. Drain immediately, plunge in ice water, and drain again. Purée basil in a blender with ½ teaspoon salt and the olive oil. Serve soup cold, drizzled with basil oil.

Quick Senegalese

From The Rainbow Cooks Soups, Salads & Specialties Cookbook
For Unexpected Guests | Serves 4

Ingredients
2 cans cream of celery soup
2 cups milk
1 tsp. curry powder
2 Tbsp. soft butter
½ cup peeled, diced tart apples

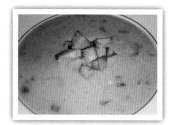

Directions
Heat celery soup and milk to boiling. Reduce heat. Beat curry powder into butter and add to soup, stirring for two minutes.
Strain and chill. Before serving, garnish with diced apples.

Chez Diana

Moroccan-Spiced Cold Tomato Soup

North African spices combine with a touch of honey and lemon in a refreshing summer soup.
From Gourmet Magazine, June 2003

1 small onion, chopped
2 tablespoons olive oil
1 teaspoon paprika
¼ teaspoon ground ginger
¼ teaspoon ground cumin
Scant ¼ teaspoon ground cinnamon
1 (14- to 16-oz) can whole tomatoes in juice, drained and juices reserved
1 ¾ cups chicken broth (14 fl oz)
2 teaspoons honey
2 tablespoons chopped fresh parsley
2 tablespoons chopped fresh cilantro
½ teaspoon fresh lemon juice, or to taste Garnish: lemon slices

Cook onion in oil with spices in a 3-quart heavy saucepan over moderate heat, stirring occasionally, until onion is softened and begins to brown, 4 to 5 minutes. Coarsely chop tomatoes and add to onion mixture with reserved juices, broth, honey, 1 Tbsp. parsley, and 1 Tbsp. cilantro, then bring to a boil. Transfer soup to a metal bowl set in a larger bowl of ice and cold water. Cool soup, stirring occasionally, until cold, 15 to 20 minutes. Stir in lemon juice and salt and pepper to taste, then stir in remaining parsley and cilantro.
Makes 4 servings or about 5 cups

Vichyssoise Soup

(Served Cold or Hot)

Ingredients

3 cups cubed potatoes
2 cups chopped onions
2 cups chicken broth
¼ tsp. salt
¼ tsp. pepper
¼ tsp. fresh basil
1 can evaporated milk
½ cup sour cream
Chives for garnish

Directions

Combine first 6 ingredients in a large saucepan. Bring to boil, cover, reduce heat and simmer for 20 minutes or until potatoes are tender. Puree until smooth. Transfer to bowl and stir in evaporated milk.

Cover and chill for 8 hours. Serve topped with sour cream and chives. May also be served hot as potato soup. Serves 6

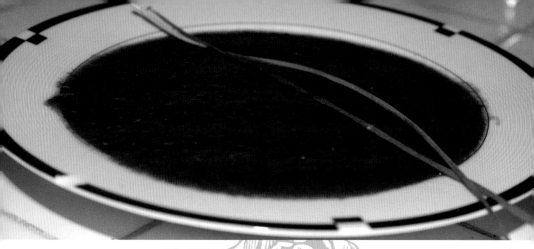

Chilled Tomato Soup

Ingredients
3 Tomatoes –chopped
½ Green Pepper – chopped
3 green onions – chopped
2 cups vegetable juice
1 Tbsp. lemon juice
½ tsp. basil, dried
¼ tsp. hot pepper sauce
1 clove garlic minced

Directions
Combine all ingredients in a large mixing bowl. Cover and chill in refrigerator for several hours.

Serves 4

Summer Strawberry Soup

Chilled summer strawberry soup is an easy summer refresher.

Ingredients

2 pints fresh strawberries
1 ½ cups of cranberry juice
Dash of cinnamon
Dash of nutmeg
1 Tbsp. honey
2 Tbsp. lemon juice
2 cups buttermilk

Directions
Wash, cap, stem, chop and puree the fresh strawberries with the cranberry juice, cinnamon and nutmeg. Sweeten with one tablespoon of honey. Add grated lemon rind and lemon juice and buttermilk. Chill overnight in a glass container.

6 Servings

Chez Diana

Bean Soup — North Woods

Adding turkey kielbasa lends this soup a rich, slow-simmered flavor even though it takes less than 30 minutes to make. Puree a portion of the recipe for a velvety consistency, and stir in fresh spinach after the soup is removed from the heat so it retains its bright color.

Cooking spray
1 cup baby carrots, halved
1 cup chopped onion
2 garlic cloves, minced
7 ounces turkey kielbasa, halved lengthwise and cut into ½-inch pieces
4 cups fat-free, less-sodium chicken broth
½ teaspoon dried Italian seasoning
½ teaspoon black pepper
2 (15.8-ounce) cans Great Northern beans, drained and rinsed
1 (6-ounce) bag fresh baby spinach leaves

Heat a large saucepan coated with cooking spray over medium-high heat. Add carrots, onion, garlic, and kielbasa; sauté 3 minutes, stirring occasionally. Reduce heat to medium; cook 5 minutes. Add the broth, Italian seasoning, pepper, and beans. Bring to a boil, reduce heat, and simmer 5 minutes. Place 2 cups of the soup in a food processor or blender, and process until smooth. Return the pureed mixture to pan. Simmer an additional 5 minutes. Remove soup from heat. Add the spinach, stirring until spinach wilts.

Yield: 5 servings
(serving size: about 1 ½ cups)

Classic Cream Soup

When you're craving a creamy vegetable soup, this recipe is sure to bowl you over. We provide the base, and you pick the produce. Cauliflower, broccoli or peas are just a few of the options you may want to explore. Whatever your choice, you'll agree this soup is good food.

Ingredients

2 cups leftover vegetables, minced
1 tbsp. onions minced
Salt and pepper
1 cup stock or vegetable soup
2 tbsp. butter
1 ½ tsp. flour
1 cup milk
1 cup cooked vegetables
Parsley

Directions

Melt butter and sauté one tbsp. of onion in it for 5 minute. Blend in flour, salt and pepper; stir in the milk slowly and then the stock. Bring to a boiling point. Add the rest of the vegetables and cook until vegetables are soft. Mix in a blender. Place some parsley on soup to garnish before serving.
Ready in 35 minutes

Chez Diana

Beer Cheese Soup

Try this beer and cheese soup recipe made with Progresso®
chicken broth from Betty Crocker. Makes 5 servings

Ingredients

½ cup butter or margarine
¾ cup finely chopped carrots
½ cup finely chopped celery
¼ cup finely chopped onion
1 cup quick-mixing flour
½ teaspoon paprika
$1/8$ teaspoon black pepper
$1/8$ teaspoon ground red pepper
  (cayenne)
3 cups Progresso® chicken broth
  (from 32-oz carton)
4 cups whipping cream
4 cups shredded sharp Cheddar
  cheese (16 oz)
1 can (12 oz) beer

Directions

In 4-quart Dutch oven, melt butter
over medium heat. Add carrots,
celery and onion; cook about 10
minutes, stirring occasionally, until
celery and onions are transparent.
Stir in flour, paprika, black pepper
and ground red pepper.

Add broth; heat to boiling over
medium heat. Boil and stir 1
minute. Reduce heat; stir in
whipping cream and cheese.
Heat until cheese is melted,
stirring occasionally. Stir in beer.

If desired, serve garnished
with popcorn.

Chez Diana

Cabbage, Cauliflower and Potato Chowder

The Washington Post, February 10, 2010

The cauliflower gives this soup depth and body, while the mustard and the garnish of caramelized cabbage elevate the taste. Recipe Source: Adapted from "The 10 Things You Need to Eat," by Dave Lieberman and Anahad O'Connor (William Morrow, 2010).

Ingredients

5 tablespoons canola oil

1 large onion, finely chopped (1 ½ cups)

2 large (about 1 pound total) russet potatoes, peeled, cut into ½-inch cubes and covered with water in a medium bowl

¾ head green cabbage, finely shredded (about 6 cups), with 2 cups reserved for garnish

½ head cauliflower, cored and coarsely chopped

1 quart low-sodium chicken or vegetable broth

1 quart water, or more as needed

2 tablespoons whole-grain mustard

Kosher salt

Freshly ground black pepper

Makes 11 cups (8 to 10 servings)

Directions

Heat 3 tablespoons of the oil in a large, heavy-bottomed pot over medium heat. Add the onion and stir to coat, then partially cover and cook for about 5 minutes, until softened. Add half of the potatoes, 4 cups of the cabbage, the cauliflower, the broth and as much water as needed to cover the ingredients. Once the liquid starts to bubble at the edges, reduce the heat to low, cover the pot and cook for 40 to 45 minutes or until the cauliflower is falling-apart tender. Remove from the heat. Use an immersion (stick) blender to puree the mixture to form a smooth soup. Place the pot of soup over low heat, then drain the remaining potato cubes and add to the soup. Cook uncovered for 20 to 30 minutes, until the potato cubes are tender. Heat the remaining 2 tablespoons of the oil in a medium nonstick skillet over medium-high heat. Add the remaining 2 cups of cabbage and cook for about 5 minutes, using tongs to toss the cabbage until it is wilted and nicely caramelized. Remove from the heat. Add the mustard to the soup, stirring to incorporate. Season with salt and pepper to taste, then divide among individual bowls. Top each portion with equal amounts of the wilted cabbage. Serve hot.

Chez Diana

Crab Bisque

From The Rainbow Cooks Soups, Salads & Specialties Cookbook
Heavenly and So Simple!

Ingredients

1 can tomato soup
1 can pea soup
2 pints cream
$^1/_3$ cup sherry, or to taste
1 lb. crab meat

Directions

Combine all ingredients.
Heat and serve.
This is a marvelous rich soup.

Serves 4

Cream of Pimiento Soup

From The Rainbow Cooks Soups, Salads & Specialties Cookbook
Different, Delicate Flavors

1 small onion, chopped
1 10 oz. jar diced pimiento, drained
3 Tbsp. butter
3 Tbsp. flour
1 ½ cup chicken stock
1 tsp. sugar
1 cup whipping cream
½ cup milk
¾ cup grated cheddar cheese
$^1/_8$ tsp. dry mustard
Salt & pepper to taste

Serves 4

Sauté onion and pimiento in butter until onion is translucent but not brown. Allow to cool. Puree. Return mixture to saucepan and gradually stir in flour. Blend with whisk. Add chicken stock and sugar. Cook over low heat, stirring constantly until soup thickens, about 15 minutes.
Add milk, cream, cheese, mustard, salt and pepper. Stir constantly, until heated through. Do not allow to boil.

Chez Diana

Cream of Peanut Soup

From The Rainbow Cooks Soups, Salads & Specialties Cookbook
Williamsburg's Famous Soup!

Ingredients

1 stalk celery, chopped
¼ onion, finely chopped
2 Tbsp. butter
1 Tbsp. flour
1 quart chicken stock
¼ lb. peanut butter
1 cup heavy cream

Directions

Sauté celery and onion in butter. Add flour and blend well over low heat. Stir in chicken stock and bring to a boil. Reduce heat and blend in peanut butter until smooth. Add cream and serve as soon as the soup is hot.

Serves 4-6

Onion Soup Gratinee

From The Rainbow Cooks Soups, Salads & Specialties Cookbook
The French Way!

Ingredients

2 quarts beef consommé
5 medium onions, sliced
2 Tbsp. butter
8 oz. vermouth or white wine,
  or half of each
Salt & pepper
1 ½ to 2 cups of grated
  Swiss cheese
Toasted French rolls,
  slice ¾ inch thick

Serves 8-10

Cut onions in half and slice thinly. Put butter & onions in a large pot. Salt lightly and cook for 10 minutes over medium heat, stirring occasionally. Raise the heat and brown the onions, stirring to keep them from burning. Add the vermouth and or wine. Cook until liquid is reduced to a little less than $1/3$. Add beef consommé. Bring to a boil and simmer for 10 minutes. Season with salt and pepper. Set oven at 325. Pour soup into individual oven proof bowls. Top with a slice of French bread, sprinkle with 2 Tbsp. Swiss cheese over bread. Bake 45-60 minutes, uncovered.

Chez Diana

Creamless Creamy Tomato Soup

From Cook's Illustrated. Published September 1, 2008.
Serves 6 to 8

Ingredients

¼ cup extra virgin olive oil, plus more for drizzling
1 medium onion, chopped medium (about 1 cup)
3 medium garlic cloves, minced or pressed through garlic press
  (about 1 tablespoon)
Pinch hot red pepper flakes (optional)
1 bay leaf
2 (28-ounce) cans whole tomatoes packed in juice
1 tablespoon brown sugar
3 large slices good-quality sandwich bread, crusts removed, torn into
  1-inch pieces
2 cups low-sodium chicken broth
2 tablespoons brandy (optional)
Table salt and ground black pepper
¼ cup chopped fresh chives

Directions

1. Heat 2 tablespoons oil in Dutch oven over medium-high heat until
   shimmering. Add onion, garlic, red pepper flakes (if using), and
   bay leaf. Cook, stirring frequently, until onion is translucent, 3 to
   5 minutes. Stir in tomatoes and
   their juice. Using potato masher,
   mash until no pieces bigger than
   2 inches remain. Stir in sugar
   and bread; bring soup to boil.
   Reduce heat to medium and cook,
   stirring occasionally, until bread
   is completely saturated and starts
   to break down, about 5 minutes.
   Remove and discard bay leaf.

2. Transfer half of soup to blender. Add 1 tablespoon oil and process until
   soup is smooth and creamy, 2 to 3 minutes. Transfer to large bowl
   and repeat with remaining soup and oil. Rinse out Dutch oven and
   return soup to pot. Stir in chicken broth and brandy (if using). Return
   soup to boil and season to taste with salt and pepper. Serve soup in
   individual bowls. Sprinkle each portion with pepper and chives and
   drizzle with olive oil.

Chez Diana

Oh So Good French Onion Soup

Recipe courtesy Rachael Ray
Prep Time: 10 min
Cook Time: 25 min

Ingredients

1 tablespoon extra-virgin olive oil
2 tablespoons butter
6 medium onions, thinly sliced
Salt and freshly ground
   black pepper
2 teaspoons fresh thyme,
   picked and chopped or
   poultry seasoning
1 bay leaf, fresh or dried
½ cup dry sherry
6 cups beef stock
4 thick slices crusty bread,
   toasted
2 ½ cups shredded
   Gruyere or Swiss cheese

Directions

Heat a deep pot over medium to medium high heat. Work next to the stove to slice onions. Add oil and butter to the pot. Add onions to the pot as you slice them.

When all the onions are in the pot, season with salt, pepper and 1 teaspoon fresh thyme. Cook onions 15 to 18 minutes, stirring frequently, until tender, sweet and caramel colored. Add bay leaf and sherry to the pot and deglaze the pan drippings. Add 6 cups stock and cover pot to bring soup up to a quick boil.

Arrange 4 small, deep soup bowls or crocks on a cookie sheet. Preheat broiler to high. Once soup reaches a boil, ladle it into bowls. Float toasted crusty bread on soup and cover each bowl with a mound of cheese. Sprinkle remaining fresh thyme on cheese and place cookie sheet with soup bowls on it under hot broiler until cheese melts and bubbles.

Sauerkraut Soup with Sausage

Recipe courtesy Emeril Lagasse, 2006
Prep Time: 10 minutes | Cook Time: 1 hr 10 minutes
Printed from FoodNetwork.com on Fri., Feb 27 2009

Ingredients

1 pound smoked sausage, such as kielbasa, diced
1 large onion, finely chopped
1 rib celery, finely chopped
1 tablespoon minced garlic
1 cup hard cider
1 (32-ounce) jar sauerkraut, drained and rinsed briefly
8 cups canned low-sodium chicken broth
1 cup peeled and cubed potatoes
3 sprigs fresh thyme
½ teaspoon freshly ground black pepper

Serves: 3 quarts soup

Directions

Heat a large soup pot over medium-high heat and add the sausage.
Cook until the sausage is caramelized and the fat is rendered, 4 to 6
minutes. Add the onions and celery and cook, stirring occasionally, until
vegetables are soft and lightly browned, about 4 minutes. Add the garlic
and cook, stirring, for 1 minute. Add the cider and cook until almost
completely reduced. Add the sauerkraut, broth, potatoes, thyme and
pepper and bring to a boil. Reduce the heat to a low simmer and cook,
stirring occasionally, until potatoes and sauerkraut are very tender and the
broth is flavorful, 45 minutes to 1 hour. Taste and adjust the seasoning, if
necessary. Serve immediately, with hot, crusty bread on the side.

Chez Diana

Spicy Hot Potato Soup

Recipe created by Cabot Creamery® on behalf of 3-A-Day of Dairy.

Ingredients

2 bacon slices
1 cup chopped carrots
1 cup chopped poblano chiles
1 cup chopped onion
2 tablespoons minced seeded
 jalapeño pepper
½ teaspoon cumin
3 minced garlic cloves
2 16-ounce cans fat free chicken broth
5 cups diced peeled baking potatoes
½ teaspoon salt
$^1/_3$ cup flour
2 ½ cups skim milk
5 ounces 50% light Jalapeño cheddar
 cheese
2 ounces 50% light cheddar cheese
$^2/_3$ cup onion

Yields: 10 1-cup servings

Directions

1. Cook bacon until crisp. Remove bacon from pan leaving 1 tablespoon drippings in pan. Crumble bacon, set aside.
2. Add carrots and next 5 ingredients to drippings. Sauté until golden brown. Stir in broth and add potato and salt. Bring to a boil. Cover, reduce heat and simmer 25 minutes or until potato is tender.
3. Combine flour and milk in a small bowl stirring with a whisk. Add to pan slowly. Cook over medium heat until thick, about 12-15 minutes. Remove from heat. Add cheddar and Jalapeño cheddar cheese, stirring until melted.
4. Serve in bowls topped with green onions and crumbled bacon.

Mushroom Soup

Soup is good food, especially when you're talking about the homemade kind.
This mouthwatering mushroom soup is sure to bowl you over.
Talk about a shroom with a view... It's a super starter for any meal.
Copyright © 2008-10 MyDailyMoment. All rights reserved.

Ingredients

8 oz. fresh mushrooms
2 tbsp. onions, chopped
1-2 garlic clove, minced
2 tbsp. butter 2-3 tbsp. flour
 (separated)
2 cups chicken broth
1 cup light cream or evaporated milk
½ tsp. salt
¼ tsp. pepper
¼ tsp. nutmeg

Directions

Cut the mushrooms into slices. Melt butter in large frying pan. Add in onions, garlic, and mushrooms. Cook until onions are soft. Blend in 2 tbsp. flour and stir. Add in the chicken broth and heat until slightly thickened while stirring frequently. Stir cream with additional 1 tbsp. flour. Add in cream to soup. Heat to thicken while stirring frequently. Serve and enjoy!

Chez Diana

Creamy Porcini Mushroom Soup

Rich, thick and flavorful, this soup is perfect for warming up a winter day.
For a nice contrast to the creamy soup, garnish servings
with crunchy croutons. From Williams-Sonoma Kitchen.

Ingredients

6 cups hot water
1.4 oz. dried porcini mushrooms
3 Tbs. olive oil
2 Tbs. unsalted butter
12 oz. white button mushrooms, sliced
8 oz. shiitake mushrooms, stemmed and sliced
1 yellow onion, chopped
2 garlic cloves, minced
1 tsp. chopped fresh thyme
1 Tbs. Champagne vinegar
4 cups low-sodium chicken or vegetable stock
  or canned broth
2 cups heavy cream
Salt and freshly ground pepper, to taste
Chopped fresh chives for garnish

Directions

In a heatproof bowl, pour the hot water over the porcini mushrooms and
soak for 30 minutes. In a large, wide-bottomed saucepan (use Dutch oven)
over high heat, warm 2 Tbs. of the oil and melt the butter. Add the button
and shiitake mushrooms and sauté, stirring occasionally, until the mushrooms
are golden and tender and the liquid has nearly evaporated, 6 to 8 minutes.
Add the remaining 1 Tbs. oil to the pan with the mushrooms, then add the
onion and garlic. Sauté, stirring occasionally, until the onions are tender and
golden, 6 to 8 minutes more. Add the thyme and sauté 1 minute more.

Strain the porcini through a fine-mesh sieve, reserving the soaking liquid and
the porcini. Add the soaking liquid to the mushroom-onion mixture along
with the vinegar, stock and cream. Bring to a simmer, reduce the heat to
medium-low and simmer for 20 minutes.

Using a stick blender, puree the soup until smooth and blended. Season with
salt and pepper. Chop the porcini coarsely and stir into the soup. Ladle into
warmed soup bowls and garnish each serving with a pinch of chopped chives.

Serves 8

Chez Diana

Make-Do Veggie Soup

Getting your minimum daily servings of vegetables can be difficult. Fortunately, this recipe provides a way to help achieve that in a single dish. Soup is also a great way to stretch your food dollars by using leftover vegetables from your refrigerator. Keep some soup base on hand, and you always can create the ultimate "make do" meal.

Ingredients

1 tablespoon extra virgin olive oil
½ large onion, chopped
3 cups reduced-fat, low-sodium chicken broth (water may be substituted)
1 can (15-oz.) no-salt-added garbanzo beans (or rinsed and drained if added salt)
1 can (28-oz.) diced plum tomatoes, with juice
1 teaspoon Cajun spice mix, with no MSG
¼ cup fresh parsley and cilantro, finely chopped, divided
Freshly ground black pepper to taste
*1 cup cooked corn kernels
*2 cups cooked collard greens
*2 cups cooked spinach
*1 cup cooked asparagus, sliced into 1 pieces
Salt to taste

Directions

Heat oil in large pot over medium-high heat. Add onions and cook until translucent, stirring occasionally.

Add broth or water, beans, tomatoes, Cajun spice mix, 2 tablespoons parsley and cilantro mix and black pepper to taste. Bring to a boil. Cover pot, reduce heat and simmer for about 15 minutes.

Add in cooked or freshly steamed vegetables. Warm through. Adjust salt to taste. Garnish with a sprinkle of parsley-cilantro mix. Serve hot.

*For convenience you can make the basic soup (all the ingredients except the veggies) and store it (refrigerate or freeze). Then when ready to serve, just warm and add vegetables on hand to make a great soup, including greens, beans, carrots, celery and broccoli. The list is almost endless – add whatever vegetables you have in your refrigerator or freezer.

Makes 6 servings (1-½ cups per serving).

Chez Diana

Hamburger Vegetable Soup

From Keyingredient.com

Ingredients

1 to 1 ½ lbs hamburger
1 medium onion, chopped
8 cups beef broth or beef bouillon
1 can chopped tomatoes with juice
4 medium potatoes, peeled and cut up
4 carrots, peeled and cut up
4 stalks celery, cut up
1 cup corn (canned or frozen)
1 cup frozen peas

Directions

Brown hamburger with chopped onion, drain off excess fat. Add beef broth and tomatoes with juice. Simmer 1 ½ hour. Add potatoes and cook 10 minutes. Add carrots and celery, cook until tender. Add corn and peas and simmer.

Salads

Chez Diana

Shrimp Salad

A great summer pasta salad!

Ingredients

2 cans shrimp
1 medium onion, chopped
3 stalks celery, chopped
3 hard boiled eggs, chopped
20 pimiento stuffed olives, chopped
3 Tbsp. oil
$1/3$ cup mayonnaise
½ box spaghetti, broken & cooked

Cook spaghetti, and cool with running water. Let stand at least one hour. Add chopped onion, celery, eggs, olives and shrimp and mix well. Stir in mayonnaise and chill well prior to serving.

Serves 4

Parsnip Salad

Recipe courtesy Dave Lieberman

Salad Ingredients

1 pound parsnips, peeled, cut in
  ½ lengthwise, then cut into
  1 ½ -inch chunks
olive oil
Salt and freshly ground black
  pepper
1 bunch watercress, thick stems
  plucked
1 Gala or Red Delicious apple,
  cored and very thinly sliced
2 small shallots, very thinly sliced

Dressing Ingredients

¼ cup apple cider vinegar
1 tablespoon whole-grain Dijon
  mustard

$1/3$ cup soybean or safflower oil
2 teaspoons superfine sugar
Preheat oven to 400 degrees F.

Toss parsnip chunks with olive oil and salt and pepper and place on a baking sheet. Roast until nicely browned, turning as needed, about 20 minutes. Let cool. Then toss with watercress, apple and shallots.

Whisk together dressing ingredients and season, to taste, with salt and pepper.

Servings 4

Chez Diana

Spinach Salad Pavilion

From The Rainbow Cooks Soups, Salads & Specialties Cookbook
This gets raves!

Ingredients

4 bunches of spinach
2 hard boiled eggs
½ lb. bacon, cooked and
  crumbled
2 oz. crumbled blue cheese
1 c. oil
1 ½ Tbsp. wine vinegar
3 cloves garlic
3 Tbsp. catsup
1 Tbsp. A-1 steak sauce
2 tsp. Worcestershire sauce
1 tsp. sugar
1 tsp. salt
¾ tsp. paprika
½ tsp. dry mustard
¼ tsp. pepper
Candied pecans

Directions

Wash spinach, dry and tear into pieces. Cook and chop the eggs.

Add bacon and eggs to spinach with cheese and refrigerate until ready to serve. Place dressing ingredients in blender and blend until dissolved. Toss salad with dressing and add pecans to serve.

Serves 4

Bean Salad with Tuna

Ingredients

¼ c. fresh parsley
2 Tbsp. olive oil
1 Tbsp. lemon juice
4 plum tomatoes
½ onion chopped
¼ tsp. salt & pepper
2 cloves crushed garlic
1 15-oz. can garbanzo beans,
  drained
1 15-oz. can white or pinto beans,
  drained
1 can tuna, drained
Lettuce leaves

Directions

Combine all ingredients except lettuce leaves. Chill.

Serve on lettuce leaves.

Serves 4

Old-Fashioned Potato Salad

Controlling Your Fat Tooth Cookbook

l egg
1 teaspoon red wine vinegar
2 teaspoons fresh lemon juice
1 teaspoon Dijon mustard
3 cloves garlic
½ teaspoon salt
1 cup olive oil
2 ¾ pounds russet potatoes, cooked
3 hard-boiled egg whites
2 whole hard-boiled eggs
2 stalks celery, finely chopped
½ cup finely chopped white onion
1 dill pickle, finely chopped salt
black pepper to taste
15 ripe black olives, pitted and halved paprika
1 tomato, cut into wedges

In a blender or food processor, combine egg, vinegar, lemon juice, mustard, garlic and salt. With machine running, gradually add olive oil, 1 tablespoon at a time. Chill at least 4 hours.

Into a large salad bowl, cut cooled, cooked potatoes in 1-inch cubes and all egg whites in 1-inch chunks. Crumble yolks over potatoes. Add celery, onion and pickle. Chill.

Just before serving, toss the potato-egg mixture with desired amount of dressing. Season to taste with salt and pepper. Sprinkle with olives, then with paprika. Garnish with tomato wedges

Marinated Peppers And Onions

Controlling Your Fat Tooth Cookbook

1 medium green pepper
1 medium red pepper
½ medium white onion
½ medium red onion
1 large tomato
1 ½ Tbsp. olive oil
1 ½ Tbsp. fresh lemon juice
1 ½ Tbsp. fresh lime juice
½ tsp. salt
¾ tsp. black pepper
½ tsp. Tabasco sauce

Cut peppers into chunks. Cut onions into chunks. Coarsely chop the tomato.

In a covered jar, combine the olive oil, lemon juice, lime juice, salt, pepper, and Tabasco sauce. Pour over the vegetables.

Chill for 2 to 3 hours before serving.

Caesar Salad

From The Rainbow Cooks Soups, Salads & Specialties Cookbook
Better than Most!

¾ cup olive oil (divided)
4 cloves garlic
2 cups bread cubes (baguette)
3 Tbsp. lemon juice
2 tsp. Worcestershire sauce
1 Tbsp. Dijon mustard
½ tsp. salt
¼ tsp. pepper
4 anchovies, chopped fine
1 head romaine lettuce
1 egg, well beaten
½ cup parmesan cheese

Directions

Wash & dry lettuce and chill while preparing dressing. Crush garlic into ½ cup of olive oil.

Heat remaining oil to fry bread cubes. Drain on paper towels. In small bowl combine lemon juice, Worcestershire sauce, salt pepper, anchovies, & mustard. Mix well.

Tear lettuce into bowl. Toss first with olive oil & garlic until well coated. Add egg and toss again. Pour in anchovy mixture and toss. Add croutons and Parmesan cheese and toss again lightly. Serve immediately.

Serves 4-6

Chez Diana

Creamy Sweet Potato Salad

You say potato-we say it's time to give this sweet treat a try.
A twist from the traditional tater salads, this one uses sweet potatoes.
Created by the my daily moment (MDM) team.

Ingredients

2 pounds sweet potatoes, peeled & cubed
1 small onion chopped
1 cup mayonnaise
½ cup packed brown sugar
1 cup walnuts
½ cup raisins

Place potatoes in large pot and fill with enough water to cover. Bring
to a boil, and cook for about 8 minutes, or until tender. Drain, and cool
slightly. In a large bowl, stir together mayonnaise and brown sugar. Stir
in the potatoes, walnuts and raisins until evenly coated. Chill for at least
one hour before serving.

Ready in 1 hour and 30 minutes.

Sauerkraut Salad

VIP Cookbook
American Cancer Society

Ingredients

1 large can sauerkraut, well drained
¹/₃ cup chopped onion
¹/₃ cup green pepper
1 2-oz. jar diced pimiento
1 cup vinegar
1 cup sugar

Directions

Mix all ingredients well and let stand at least 24 hours before serving.
This salad will keep as long as it lasts.

Serves 10

Chez Diana

Marinated Carrot Salad

From Exquisito, The Women's Guild Cookbook
Union Church, Tegucigalpa, Honduras 1981

Ingredients

2 lbs. carrots, peeled and slices
2 onions, chopped
1 medium green or red pepper, chopped
1 can tomato soup
²/₃ cup white vinegar
²/₃ cup sugar
½ cup salad oil
1 tsp. Worcestershire sauce
1 tsp. prepared mustard
½ tsp. salt

Directions

Cook carrots for 8 – 10 minutes. Drain. Combine carrots, chopped onions and chopped peppers. Stir remaining ingredients and pour over vegetables. Let stand or chill for several hours before serving.

Corn and Tomato Salad

PREP AND COOK TIME: About 30 minutes
MAKES 4 to 6 servings

½ cup chopped red onion
1 tablespoon olive oil
4 cups fresh corn kernels
2 cups cherry tomatoes, rinsed, stemmed, and halved if larger
  than ¾ inch
¼ cup slivered fresh basil leaves
3 tablespoons sherry vinegar or red wine vinegar
Salt and pepper
2 ounces fresh chevre (goat) cheese, crumbled

1. In a 10- to 12-inch frying pan over medium-high heat, stir onion in olive oil until limp, 5 to 7 minutes. Add corn and stir often just until tender to bite, 5 to 6 minutes.
2. Pour mixture into a wide serving bowl and stir in tomatoes, basil, and vinegar. Add salt and pepper to taste

Sprinkle goat cheese over salad; serve warm or at room temperature.

Chez Diana

Tomato Salad Monterey

A find of my sister, Kay, who lives close to Monterey in California!
This is a great salad for picnics.

Ingredients

3 lbs. fresh tomatoes, diced
8 oz. Monterey Jack cheese, diced or shredded
2 (4 oz.) Blue cheese, crumbled
2 Avocados, diced
½ cup red onion, diced
1 Teaspoon salt (optional)
½ teaspoon pepper
1 cup Thousand Island Dressing (Marie's is good)
6 slices bacon, crumbled
8 oz. Macaroni, cooked, drained, and cooled

Fold all ingredients into cooled pasta. Chill.

Makes 6-8 servings

Rachel Ray's Tomato Salad

Ingredients

8 plum tomatoes—seeded, quartered and thinly sliced
1 medium red onion, quartered and thinly sliced
1 cup fresh basil leaves, cut into thin strips
½ cup flat-leaf parsley (a couple
of generous handfuls), chopped
⅓ cup extra-virgin olive oil
  (EVOO), eyeball it
Coarse salt and freshly ground
  pepper

In a medium bowl, toss
together the tomatoes, onion,
basil and parsley and dress with
the extra virgin olive oil. Season
to taste with salt and pepper.

Chez Diana

Chick Pea Salad

Ingredients

3 c. cooked or canned chick peas
¼ c. chopped onion
2 tbsp. chopped pimiento (raw or cooked)
2 tbsp. chopped (not grated) raw carrot
Salad oil and vinegar
2 tbsp. chopped green pepper
3 tbsp. mayonnaise
1 ½ tsp. mustard
Salt to taste

Directions

Cook chick peas until soft, but do not overcook. Chick peas should be soaked overnight as beans. Chick peas can be cooked in the pressure cooker after soaking. Drain soaking water and cover well with fresh water; cook 25 to 30 minutes under pressure, then let the pressure go down without putting under cold water. Drain. Mix together with all the other ingredients. This salad will keep for some time in the refrigerator and is high in protein. With the chopped red pimiento it makes a colorful salad for summer meals or picnics. Canned chick peas are very good in this and make a quick and easy salad

Chicken, Pear, and Blue Cheese Salad

© BHG Better Homes and Garden <http://www.bhg.com>
Start to Finish: 15 min.

Ingredients

6 cups packaged torn mixed greens or mesclun
10 to 12 ounces roasted or grilled chicken breast, sliced
¾ cup bottled reduced-calorie or regular blue cheese salad dressing
2 pears, cored and sliced
Freshly ground black pepper (optional)

Directions

In a large bowl, combine the torn greens, chicken, and salad dressing; toss gently to coat. Divide among four large salad bowls or dinner plates. Arrange pear slices on top of salads. Sprinkle with pepper, if desired.

Makes 4 servings

Egg Salad

2 hard boiled eggs, chopped
1 tbsp mayonnaise
1 tbsp mustard (I use yellow)
3 tbps chopped onion
1 or 2 tbsp chopped dill pickle
½ tsp of celery seed
½ tsp of tarragon

Cracked black pepper to taste
¼ tsp of dill weed

Mix well and chill slightly
before serving.

Serves 1, double for 2

Layered Caribbean Chicken Salad

Prep Time: 30 min Total Time: 30 min

Salad

3 cups shredded romaine lettuce
2 cups cubed cooked chicken
1 cup shredded Monterey Jack cheese (4 oz)
1 can (15 oz) black beans, drained, rinsed
1 ½ cups diced peeled ripe fresh mango
½ cup chopped seeded plum (Roma) tomatoes (1 to 2 medium)
1 cup shredded Cheddar cheese (4 oz)
½ cup thinly sliced green onions (8 medium)
½ cup cashews

In small bowl, mix dressing ingredients until well blended. In 3- or
4-quart clear glass serving bowl, layer salad ingredients in order listed,
except cashews. Spoon dressing evenly over salad; sprinkle cashews
over top.

Dressing

1 container (6 oz) Yoplait® Original 99% Fat Free piña colada yogurt
1 ½- 2 tablespoons lime juice
1 teaspoon Caribbean jerk seasoning (dry)

Makes: 6 servings (1 ½ cups each)

Chez Diana

Rainbow Fruit Salad

I use different fruit – such as apples, pears, peaches, oranges.

Ingredients
1 large mango, peeled and chopped
2 cups blueberries
2 nectarines, unpeeled & sliced
2 cups strawberries, diced
2 cups seedless grapes
2 bananas, peeled and diced
1 kiwi, peeled and diced
Honey Orange Sauce
$^1/_3$ cup orange juice
2 Tbsp. lemon juice

1 ½ Tbsp. honey
¼ tsp. ground ginger
Dash of nutmeg

Directions
Prepare the fruit. Combine all sauce ingredients and mix. Just before serving, pour honey orange sauce over fruit.

Serves 12

Pasta Salad with Lemon and Peas

Small shell or bow-tie pasta is dressed in a light, lemony mayonnaise with green onions, fresh basil, and baby peas. By: Good Housekeeping
Total Time: 20 min

Ingredients
1 pound bow-tie or small shell pasta
Salt
1 package (10 ounces) frozen baby peas
2 lemons
$^2/_3$ cup milk
½ cup light mayonnaise
¼ teaspoon coarsely ground black pepper
1 cup loosely packed fresh basil leaves, chopped
4 green onions, thinly sliced

8 Servings

Directions
In large saucepot, cook pasta in boiling salted water as label directs, adding frozen peas during last 2 minutes of cooking time. Drain pasta and peas; rinse with cold water and drain well. Meanwhile, from lemons, grate 1 tablespoon peel and squeeze 3 tablespoons juice. In large bowl, with wire whisk, mix lemon peel and juice with milk, mayonnaise, pepper, basil, green onions, and salt until blended. Add pasta and peas to mayonnaise dressing; toss to coat well. Cover and refrigerate up to two days if not serving right away.

Strawberry Salad

Have we got a berry good salad for you? No need to draw straws, only
strawberries. Combine romaine and spinach for a super salad that won't
leaf you high and dry. It's the perfect way to start or finish a summer meal.
PREP TIME 15 Min | READY IN 15 Min

Ingredients

1 head romaine lettuce - rinsed,
   dried, and chopped
2 bunches fresh spinach -
   chopped, washed and dried
1 pint fresh strawberries, sliced
1 Bermuda onion, sliced
½ cup mayonnaise
2 tbsp. white wine vinegar
$1/3$ cup white sugar
¼ cup milk
2 tbsp. poppy seeds

Directions

In a large salad bowl, combine the
romaine, spinach, strawberries and
sliced onion.
In a jar with a tight fitting lid,
combine the mayonnaise, vinegar,
sugar, milk and poppy seeds.
Shake well and pour the dressing
over salad. Toss until evenly
coated.

Serves 6

Chez Diana

Field Greens with Glazed Walnuts, Pears & Gorgonzola

Sweet and crunchy Emerald Original Glazed Walnuts make this refreshing salad a delightful luncheon entree or welcome first course for dinner. It's quick and easy to prepare, and is sure to win compliments from family and guests. Emerald Original Glazed Walnuts are also delicious additions for appetizers, desserts and stir fry dishes.

Salad

1 cup Emerald® Original Glazed Walnuts
6 cups baby salad greens washed and dried
2 ripe Cornice or Anjou pears, quartered, cored and thinly sliced
½ cup (4 ounces) crumbled Gorgonzola cheese
Freshly ground black pepper

Dressing

1 tablespoon balsamic vinegar
½ teaspoon Dijon mustard
½ teaspoon salt

¼ teaspoon freshly ground pepper
3 to 4 tablespoons olive oil

To make dressing, in a large salad bowl whisk together vinegar, mustard, salt and pepper. Drizzle in oil, whisking until combined. Add greens and pears and gently toss together until lightly coated with dressing. Sprinkle cheese, glazed walnuts and pepper over salad. Serve immediately.

Serves 4 to 6

Fruit Salad with Poppy Seed Dressing

Cooking.com | 4-6 servings | Recipe reprinted by permission of Crisco

Ingredients

1 pear, cored and sliced
1 apple, cored and sliced
1 banana, peeled and sliced
1 orange, peeled and sectioned
1/3 cup Crisco Oil
2 tablespoons lime juice
2 tablespoons honey
½ teaspoon soy sauce
½ teaspoon poppy seed
¼ teaspoon ground ginger
¼ teaspoon dry mustard
Dash salt

Directions

Combine pear, apple, banana and orange in medium serving bowl. Blend remaining ingredients in small mixing bowl. Pour over fruit. Toss to coat. Serve immediately.

Roasted Red Pepper, Tuna and Bean Salad

The Washington Post, May 23, 2012 | Serves 4

Ingredients

7 oz tuna in water, drained
1 15.5 oz can Great Northern
  beans, drained (I use Navy beans)
1/3 cup Vidalia onion, chopped
1 rib celery, chopped (1/3 cup)
1/3 cup roasted red bell pepper,
  chopped
Juice of 2 lemons
2 Tbsp. olive oil
3 Tbsp. vinegar
Salt
Freshly ground black pepper

Directions

Flake the tuna into medium-size pieces. Combine the tuna, beans, onion, celery, roasted bell pepper, lemon juice, oil, vinegar, salt and pepper in a medium bowl. Stir to combine. Taste, and adjust seasoning and/or oil as needed.

Sunday Morning

NOTES

...ing Syracuse Tops ...etown in Lacrosse

...rs hit
... goalie **John**
... 8-5
...sterday at
... of 2,942
...dskins
...ranked
...til the

first shot of the game. Syracuse responded with the last three goals. **Matt Abbott** scored the go-ahead goal 16 seconds after Cochran's equalizer, and **Stephen Keogh** added his fourth goal and Abbott his second.

Aside from a four-goal third period, though, Georgetown's offense was stymied. **Andrew Brancaccio** was the Hoyas' only multiple-goal scorer with two.

In the second game of the doubleheader, the Georgetown women, ranked seventh, fell 15-4 to No. 1 Northwestern, the four-time defending national champion. In other men's games, **Grant Catalino** ...ored four goals in a 9-7 win for No. ...aryland (4-1) at Towson (1-3), **Andy Warner**'s three goals ...d No. 14 Navy (4-2, 1-1 Patriot ...e) to a 14-9 home win over ...te (2-2, 0-1).

— *Lacy Lusk*

TELEVISION AND RADIO LISTINGS

HOCKEY

12:30 p.m.	**Boston at New York Rangers**	» WRC (Channel 4), ...BAL (Channel
3 p.m.	**Pittsburgh at Washington**	» Comca... ...ED (820 AM,
	1500 AM)	

PROFESSIONAL BASKETBALL

3:30 p.m.	**Phoenix at San Antonio**	» WJLA (Cha...

MEN'S COLLEGE BASKETBALL

Noon	**Patriot League semifinal, Army at A...**	...rican » Comcast SportsN...
Noon	**Purdue at Michigan State**	» WUSA (Cha... ...WJZ (Channel 13)
2 p.m.	**Virginia Tech at Florida State**	» WDCA (Channel 20), WNUV...
	WWXT (92.7 FM), WWXX (94.3 FM), WT... ...M)	
2 p.m.	**Missouri Valley tournament final, Illinois Sta...**	
	WUSA (Channel 9), WJZ (Channel 13)	
2 p.m.	**America East tournament semifinal, U...**	
3 p.m.	**CAA tournament semifinal, Old Do...**	
	Comcast Network	
4 p.m.	**Duke at North Carolina** » ...	
	(1260 AM)	
5 p.m.	**America East to...**	
	» MASN	
5:30 p.m.	**CAA tou...**	
	Netw...	
6 p.m.		
7 p...		

Breakfast/Brunch

Salmon Skillet Puff

From Better Homes and Gardens "Brunches & Breakfasts Cookbook" Similar to soufflé only made in a skillet. It starts on the stovetop and finishes in the oven.

Ingredients

¹/₈ tsp. salt
½ cup milk
1 Tbsp. butter or margarine
2 tsp. all purpose flour
4 eggs
1 6-¾ oz. can salmon, drained
  & flaked
2 Tbsp. diced drained pimientos
2 Tbsp. margarine or butter
¼ cup plain yogurt
¼ cup mayonnaise
¼ tsp. shredded lemon peel
¼ tsp. dried dill weed

Preheat oven to 325 degrees.
In small saucepan cook onion in butter or margarine till tender but not brown. Stir in flour and salt. Add milk all at once. Cook and stir until mixture is thick and bubbly. Set aside.

Separate eggs. In a small mixing bowl beat the egg yolks. Gradually stir into the thickened mixture. In a large bowl, beat the egg whites until stiff peaks form. Gradually pour thickened yolk mixture over egg whites, gently folding to combine. Fold in salmon and pimiento.

In 10 inch ovenproof skillet, heat margarine until a drop of water sizzles. Pour in egg mixture, mounding it higher at the sides. Cook uncovered over low heat for 5 minutes or until puffed and set on the edges. Immediately place skillet in 325 degree oven. Bake for 10-12 minutes or until a knife inserted near the center comes out clean.

For sauce, in a bowl stir together the yogurt, mayonnaise, lemon peel and dill weed. Serve sauce over each serving of the salmon puff.

Serves 4

Chocolate French Toast

Ingredients

2 eggs
½ cup chocolate-flavored milk
2 tablespoons margarine or butter
4-6 slices bread
Sifted powdered sugar

Crack the eggs into the mixing bowl. Beat with eggbeater or fork till the yolks and whites are mixed. Add chocolate-flavored milk. Beat till well mixed. Pour egg mixture into a pie plate. Put half of the margarine or butter in a skillet on medium-high heat. Dip one slice of the bread into the egg mixture. Turn the bread over to coat the other side. Put the coated bread in the skillet. Repeat with another slice of bread. Cook till the bottoms are brown. To see if the bottoms are brown, lift the bread with a pancake turner and peek underneath. Turn bread over with the pancake turner. Cook till the other side is brown. Remove bread from the skillet with the pancake turner. Put the remaining margarine or butter in the skillet. Repeat with the remaining bread and egg mixture. Sprinkle French toast with powdered sugar.

Grilled Cream Cheese Sandwich

From Joanne Fluke's "Blueberry Muffin Murder"

Ingredients

For each sandwich you will need
2 slices of bread (white, wheat, French, any type you like)
1 package of cream cheese
Softened butter

Directions

Preheat the frying pan. Butter the bread. Place in pan. Cut cream cheese ½ inch thick. Cover the bread surface with cheese and top with second piece of bread buttered side up. Fry sandwich until it is golden on both sides. Remove from pan and cut sandwich in four pieces to serve.

Chez Diana

Breakfast Dish

Ingredients

8 eggs beaten
6 slices of bread, cubed
1 lb. sausage, cooked & crumbled
2 c. milk
½ tsp. salt
1 tsp. dry mustard
1 c. cheddar cheese, grated

Directions

In a greased 9" X 13" dish, put the bread cubes. Sprinkle the cheese and sausage over the bread cubes. Whisk together the eggs, salt, milk, and mustard (we don't use the salt). Pour over the rest of the ingredients. Cover with plastic wrap and refrigerate over night. Cook the next morning at 350 degrees for 35 minutes.

Serves 4-6 people

Ham and Corn Frittata

Love hearty breakfasts? Whip up a frittata. You just mix the eggs and all the extras, like cheese and veggies, and cook them in a skillet.
Prep Time:10 min | Start to Finish: 30 min | Makes: 6 servings

Ingredients

8 eggs
½ cup diced provolone or mozzarella cheese (2 oz)
½ cup Green Giant® Niblets® frozen whole kernel corn or fresh corn kernels
2 tablespoons chopped fresh chives
2 tablespoons chopped fresh parsley
¼ teaspoon salt
¼ teaspoon pepper
½ cup diced cooked ham (2 oz)
1 tablespoon butter or margarine

Directions

In medium bowl, beat all ingredients except ham and butter with fork or wire whisk until well mixed. Stir in ham. In 10-inch nonstick skillet, melt butter over medium-low heat. Pour egg mixture into skillet. Cover; cook 14 to 17 minutes or until eggs are set in center and light brown on bottom. Turn upside down onto serving plate.

Chez Diana

Ham, Egg and Cheese Bake

Silvana Nardone From Every Day with Rachael Ray September 2008

Ingredients

4-6 slices bread cubed
8 oz. deli ham chopped
2 ½ cups Monterey jack cheese, divided
3 Tbsp. chopped fresh chives, divided
6 large eggs (I use 2 eggs and ½ c. eggbeaters)
½ c. milk (I use ¼ c.)
¼ tsp. salt
½ tsp. pepper
2 plum tomatoes, sliced

Directions

Preheat oven to 350 degrees. Grease a 2-qt. ovenproof casserole. Layer the bread, the ham, 2 cups of cheese, and 2 Tbsp. chives in the dish. In medium bowl, whisk the eggs, milk and salt and pepper. Pour egg mixture over bread in dish. Top with tomato slices in an even layer. Bake until nearly set, 30 minutes. Sprinkle remaining cheese and chives on top and bake until golden.

Serves 4

Chez Diana

Sticky Bun French Toast

From Sunset Magazine

At Castle Marne, the bed-and-breakfast operated by Diane and
Jim Peiker, this baked French toast with a sticky bun topping is very
popular with the guests. It's also very easy to make. You can start
it the night before and have it ready to bake in the morning.

Ingredients

About ¼ cup ($^1/_8$ lb.) butter or margarine
1 sourdough baguette (8 oz.), cut
  diagonally in 1-inch-thick slices
  (I use French bread)
5 large eggs
1 cup half-and-half
  (I use evaporated milk)
1 cup milk
¼ teaspoon ground nutmeg
1 teaspoon ground cinnamon
1 teaspoon vanilla
½ cup firmly packed brown sugar
1 tablespoon light corn syrup
½ cup chopped pecans or walnuts

Yield: Makes 4 to 6 servings

Directions

1. Lightly butter a 9- by 13-inch pan. Lay baguette slices on a cut side
   in a single layer in pan, squeezing if needed to make them fit. In a
   blender or in a bowl with a whisk, whirl or beat eggs, half-and-half,
   milk, nutmeg, cinnamon, and vanilla to blend well. Pour egg mixture
   over bread to moisten evenly. Cover and refrigerate at least 8 or up to
   24 hours.

2. In a 1- to 2-quart pan over medium heat, stir 1/4 cup butter with
   brown sugar, corn syrup, and pecans until butter melts. Uncover bread
   mixture and spread slices evenly with the butter mixture, using all of it.

3. Bake, uncovered, in a 350° oven until topping is browned and bubbly,
   about 45 minutes. Scoop portions into bowls to serve.

Chez Diana

Farmer's Omelet

Ingredients

½ lb. sausage or diced ham
2 Tbsp. butter
2 cups diced uncooked potatoes
¼ cup onion, finely chopped
¼ cup chopped parsley
6 eggs
½ tsp. salt
Pepper to taste
2 Tbsp. milk
½ shredded cheddar cheese

Directions

Cook and drain sausage and set aside. Melt butter in a frying pan. Add onions and potatoes and cook, covered over medium heat for 20 minutes, stirring to brown evenly until potatoes are tender and golden brown. Add sausage; heat through, then sprinkle with parsley (if using). Beat eggs, milk, salt and pepper together in a bowl. Pour over the potato mixture. Cover pan and cook 10 minutes OR until eggs are almost set. Uncover pan and check often and with a spatula, lift around edge of eggs and allow egg mixture to run under omelet during cooking. Sprinkle with cheese. Cover and cook until cheese melts.
Cut into wedges and serve.
Serves 4

Hard Boiled Egg
& Sausage Casserole
The Washington Post – T C of Laurel

Ingredients

Butter for casserole dish
6 hard cooked eggs, sliced
1 pound bulk sausage, cooked
1 ½ cups sour cream
½ cups bread crumbs
1 ½ cups shredded cheddar
  cheese

Butter the bottom of a 2 quart casserole dish. Layer sliced eggs in the dish. In a frying pan, crumble and cook the sausage meat. Drain well. Combine the sour cream with the sausage and mix well. Pour over eggs. Combine bread crumbs and cheddar cheese. Sprinkle over sausage mixture. Bake at 350 degrees until bubbling (about 30 minutes).

Chez Diana

Stuffed French Toast

For a different taste, I use Irish Cream instead of regular milk

8 slices of bread
8 oz. package of cream cheese, softened
6 eggs (I use 3 eggs and ¾ cup egg beaters)
1 cup milk (or Irish Cream)
3 Tbsp. butter
Powdered sugar

Heat butter in frying pan. Whip eggs and milk. Dip bread slices in mixture and place in pan. Brown on one side. Turn over & place a slice of cream cheese on 4 slices. Place a second slice browned side down on top of cream cheese. Finish browning. Dust with powdered sugar. Serve with syrup or honey.

Artichoke Bites

From Food Network Kitchens

Ingredients

1 slice whole wheat bread, crusts removed
¼ teaspoon dried oregano leaves
1 (6-ounce) jar oil-marinated artichoke hearts, drained, rinsed, and chopped
1/3 cup freshly grated Parmesan (about 1 ¼ ounce)
2 tablespoons chopped fresh flat-leaf parsley
1 tablespoon extra-virgin olive oil
½ small onion, chopped
1 clove garlic, chopped
½ teaspoon kosher salt
¼ teaspoon red pepper flakes
3 large eggs

Yield: 6 servings

Directions

Preheat the oven to 375 degrees F. Lightly butter or spray a 6-cup nonstick muffin tin. Toast the bread slice until crisp. Cool and cut the toast into small pieces into a medium-size bowl and add the oregano, artichoke hearts, cheese, and parsley.
Heat the oil in a small skillet over medium heat, add the onion, garlic, salt, and red pepper flakes, and cook until soft, about 5 minutes. Stir into the artichoke mixture.
Lightly beat the eggs in a small bowl until foamy, stir into the artichoke mixture; spoon a ¼ cup of the mixture into each of the muffin cups. Cook until lightly puffed, golden, and just set in the center, about 17 to 20 minutes. Let cool on a rack for about 5 minutes, then remove the artichoke bites from the pan and serve warm.

Pancakes with Banana-Walnut Syrup

Pancakes

2 cups Bisquick
½ c. oats
2 Tbsp. packed brown sugar
1 ¼ cup milk
2 eggs

Heat griddle to 375. Grease griddle with vegetable oil (or spray with cooking spray before heating). In medium bowl, stir all pancake ingredients with whisk until blended. For each pancake, pour ¼ cup batter unto hot griddle. Cook until edges are dry. Turn; cook other side until golden. Serve with warm syrup.

Banana-Walnut Syrup

2 Tbsp. butter
¼ cup walnuts, chopped
2 bananas, sliced
1 cup maple flavored syrup

In 1 ½ qt. saucepan, melt butter over medium heat. Add walnuts, cook stirring occasionally, just until walnuts begin to brown. Add bananas, stir to coat with butter. Stir in syrup. Reduce heat to low; cook until warm. Keep warm while making pancakes.

Serves 6

Chez Diana

Spicy Apple Pancakes
with Cider Sauce

1987 Annual Southern Living Cookbook,
page 224 Marie Wiker, Pineville, Louisiana

Pancakes

2 cups Bisquick
½ tsp. ground cinnamon
1 egg, beaten
1 ⅓ cups milk
¾ cup shredded apple

Combine Bisquick and cinnamon
in a bowl. Combine egg and
milk; stir into dry ingredients until
smooth. Stir in shredded apple.
For each pancake spoon about
¼ cup batter onto a hot lightly
greased griddle. Turn pancakes
when tops are covered with
bubbles and edges are brown.
Serve with cider sauce.
Yields 13 4-inch pancakes.

Cider Sauce

½ cup sugar
1 Tbsp. cornstarch
⅛ tsp. cinnamon
⅛ tsp. nutmeg
1 cup apple cider/juice
1 Tbsp. lemon juice
2 Tbsp. butter or margarine

Combine first 4 ingredients in a
heavy saucepan; gradually add
apple cider/juice and lemon juice.
Cook over medium heat, stirring
constantly, until mixture boils.
Cook 1 minute, stirring constantly.
Remove from heat; stir in butter.
Yields 1 ¼ cups.

Ford Family Waffles

From "The White House Cook Book"
The best waffles I ever tasted.

Ingredients

1 ¼ cups cake flour
3 teaspoons baking powder
½ teaspoon salt
2 tablespoons confectioners' sugar
1 ½ cups milk, at room temperature
½ teaspoon vanilla extract
3 egg yolks
5 tablespoons melted butter
3 egg whites, at room temperature
1 pint fresh strawberries, lightly
   dusted with granulated sugar
1 pint sour cream

Directions

Into a large mixing bowl, sift together flour, baking powder, salt, and sugar. Using the back of a wooden spoon, make a deep well in the center of the dry ingredients.

In a separate mixing bowl, combine milk, vanilla, egg yolks, and melted butter. Pour rapidly into the center of the dry ingredients, and combine quickly, using a wire whisk.

In a clean, dry bowl, beat the egg whites until stiff but not dry. Fold into batter. Transfer batter to a pitcher for easy pouring.

Heat a waffle iron to medium-hot temperature. Pour in batter until grid is two-thirds full.

Close the lid of the waffle iron and bake for minutes, or until steam stops emerging and waffle is golden brown. Remove gently, using a fork. (Waffles should not stick to a well-seasoned iron, but if they do, add a little melted butter to the batter, not to the iron.)

Repeat baking process to make 5 more waffles.

Serve hot, accompanied by bowls of sweetened strawberries and sour cream, or a pitcher of maple syrup and a crock of whipped butter.

Bacon and Egg Puffs

Prep time: 10 minutes.
Cook time: 20 minutes

Ingredients

$^1/_3$ cup small cubes sharp Cheddar cheese (or any cheese)
3 strips Oscar Mayer Thick Cut Precooked Bacon, torn into pieces
1 large croissant, cut into ½-inch squares
1 green onion, sliced
3 eggs, beaten
¼ cup half & half or milk
pepper to taste

Makes: 6 servings

Directions

Preheat oven to 400°F. Spray 6 muffin or custard cups with nonstick cooking spray.
In a medium bowl, stir together cheese, bacon, croissant and green onions; spoon equal amounts into muffin cups. Beat together eggs and half & half in a small bowl; season lightly with pepper, then pour over croissant mixture.
Bake for 20 minutes, or until golden brown.

Makes 6 small servings.

Santa Fe Egg Bake

A hearty bake of traditional breakfast favorites with the flavor & romance of Santa Fe.

4 cups frozen southern-style hash brown potatoes
1 can (15 oz) Progresso® black beans, drained, rinsed
1 cup fresh or frozen whole kernel corn
1 cup frozen stir-fry bell peppers and onions, from 1-pound bag
2 cups shredded Colby-Monterey Jack cheese (8 ounces)
2 tablespoons chopped fresh cilantro
8 eggs
1 ¼ cups milk
½ teaspoon salt
¼ teaspoon ground red pepper

Spray rectangular baking dish, 11 x 7 x 1 ½ inches, with cooking spray. Mix potatoes, beans, corn and stir-fry peppers and onions in baking dish. Sprinkle with cheese and cilantro. Beat eggs, milk, salt and red pepper until well blended. Pour evenly over potato mixture. Cover and refrigerate at least 2 hours but no longer than 24 hours. Heat oven to 350°F. Bake uncovered 55 to 60 minutes or until knife inserted in center comes out clean. Let stand 5 minutes before cutting

Chez Diana

Best Ever Banana Muffins

From Cooks.com

2 ¼ cups all purpose or white whole wheat flour
½ teaspoon salt
2 teaspoons baking powder
½ teaspoon ground cinnamon
½ cup melted butter
2 cups firmly packed brown sugar
2 large eggs
2 large extra ripe bananas (peeled and mashed)
1 teaspoon vanilla
½ cup walnuts or pecans, chopped

In a large bowl sift together the flour, salt, baking powder, and cinnamon. In a separate bowl, mix the butter and brown sugar. Stir in the eggs, then add the bananas. Stir in the vanilla. Combine the liquid mixture with the dry ingredients, stirring together only until mixed. Stir in chopped nuts. Transfer the batter into greased muffin cups, filling ⅔ full. Bake in a 350°F oven for 25-30 minutes or until a toothpick inserted in a center comes out clean.

Chez Diana

Low Fat Banana Bread

Created by The MDM Team, Sunday, October 28, 2007
Very easy and a great way to use leftover bananas! This bread is surprisingly moist and has a wonderful flavor. For a little variation, add nuts or raisins.
READY IN 1 Hr 5 Min

Ingredients

1 ½ cups all-purpose flour
¾ cup white sugar
1 ¼ tsp. baking powder
½ tsp. baking soda
½ tsp. ground cinnamon
2 egg whites
1 cup banana, mashed
¼ cup applesauce

Directions

Preheat oven to 350 degrees. Lightly grease an 8x4 inch loaf pan.
In a large bowl, stir together flour, sugar, baking powder, baking soda and cinnamon. Add egg whites, bananas and applesauce; stir just until combined. Pour batter into prepared pan.

Bake in preheated oven for 50 to 55 minutes, until a toothpick inserted into center of loaf comes out clean. Turn out onto wire rack and allow to cool before slicing.

Chez Diana

Seafood Quiche

From Kraft Kitchens
Prep Time: 15 minTotal Time: 55 min

1 pkg. (8 oz.) PHILADELPHIA
  Cream Cheese, softened
1 can (6 oz.) crabmeat, drained,
  flaked (can use tuna, shrimp,
  salmon)
4 eggs
½ cup milk
½ cup sliced green onions
½ tsp. dill weed
½ tsp. lemon pepper seasoning
1 baked deep dish pastry shell
  (9 inch)

PREHEAT oven to 350°F. Mix all ingredients except pastry shell with electric mixer on medium speed until well blended.

POUR into pastry shell.

BAKE 40 minutes or until knife inserted in center comes out clean. Let stand 10 minutes before serving.

Makes: 8 servings

No-Fuss Tuna Quiche

© StarKist® Tuna

Ingredients

1 unbaked 9-inch deep-dish
  pastry shell
1 ½ cups low-fat milk
3 extra-large eggs
$^1/_3$ cup chopped green onions
1 tablespoon chopped drained
  pimiento
1 teaspoon dried basil leaves,
  crushed
½ teaspoon salt
1 (3-ounce) STARKIST Flavor Fresh
  Pouch® Tuna (Albacore or Chunk
  Light)
½ cup (2 ounces) shredded low-fat
  Cheddar cheese
8 spears (4 inches each) broccoli

Makes 8 servings

Preheat oven to 450°F. Bake pastry shell for 5 minutes; remove to rack to cool. Reduce oven temperature to 325°F.For filling, in large bowl whisk together milk & eggs. Stir in onions, pimiento, basil & salt. Fold in tuna & cheese. Pour into prebaked pastry shell. Bake at 325°F for 30 minutes. Meanwhile, in sauccpan, steam broccoli spears over simmering water for 5 minutes. Drain; set aside. After 30 minutes baking time, arrange broccoli spears, spoke-fashion, over quiche. Bake 25 to 35 minutes more or until knife inserted 2 inches from center comes out clean. Let stand for 5 minutes. Cut into 8 wedges, centering broccoli spear in each wedge. Note If desired, 1 cup chopped broccoli can be added to the filling before baking.

Tomato, Basil & Garlic Quiche

A real man's quiche!
Preparation Time: 10 mins | Cooking Time: 1 hr | Servings: 8 servings

1 unbaked 9-inch (4-cup volume) pie shell
1 ½ cups sour cream
½ cup Evaporated Milk
½ cup (2 oz.) grated Parmesan cheese, divided
4 large eggs, lightly beaten
¼ teaspoon salt
¼ teaspoon ground black pepper
3 tablespoons seasoned dry breadcrumbs
1 teaspoon dried basil leaves, crushed, or 1 tablespoon chopped fresh basil
3 cloves garlic, finely chopped
1 ¾ cups fresh or canned diced tomatoes, drained
¼ cup chopped ripe olives

PREHEAT oven to 350° F.

WHISK sour cream, evaporated milk, ¼ cup cheese, eggs, salt and pepper in medium bowl; pour into pie shell. Combine remaining cheese, breadcrumbs, basil and garlic in small bowl; sprinkle over sour cream mixture. Top with tomatoes and olives. BAKE for 50 to 60 minutes or until knife inserted near center comes out clean. Cool on wire rack for 5 minutes before serving.

Mushroom & Sausage Quiche

These crustless mini quiches are like portable omelets.

8 oz. turkey breakfast sausage
1 tsp. extra virgin olive oil
8 oz. mushrooms, sliced
¼ c. sliced scallions
¼ c. shredded Swiss cheese
1 tsp. freshly ground pepper
5 eggs
3 egg whites
1 cup 1% milk

Position rack in center of oven; preheat oven to 325 degrees. Coat a nonstick muffin tin with cooking spray. Heat a large nonstick skillet over medium-high heat. Add sausage and cook until golden brown, 6 to 8 minutes. Transfer to a bowl to cool. Add oil to the pan. Add mushrooms and cook, stirring, until golden brown, 5 to 7 minutes. Transfer mushrooms to the bowl with the sausage. Let cool for 5 minutes. Stir in scallions, cheese and pepper. Whisk eggs, egg whites and milk in medium bowl. Divide the egg mixture evenly among the prepared muffin cups. Sprinkle a heaping tablespoon of the sausage mixture into each cup. Bake until the tops are just beginning to brown, 25 minutes. Let cool on a wire rack for 5 minutes. Place a rack on top of the pan, flit it over to turn the quiches out onto the rack. Turn upright and cool completely.

Chez Diana

Easy Cheese and Bacon Quiche

A press-in-the-pan Bisquick® crust. Serving quiche has just become
extra easy. © 2007 ®/ TM General Mills All Rights Reserved
Prep Time: 15 min; Start to Finish: 55 min; Makes: 8 servings

1 ¼ cups Original Bisquick® mix
¼ cup butter or margarine,
  softened
2 tablespoons boiling water
1 package (6 oz) sliced Canadian
  bacon, chopped
1 cup shredded Swiss cheese (4 oz)
4 medium green onions, thinly
  sliced (¼ cup)
1 ½ cups half-and-half
3 eggs
½ teaspoon salt
¼ teaspoon ground red pepper
  (cayenne)

Heat oven to 400°F. Grease bottom and side of 9-inch pie plate with shortening. Stir Bisquick and butter until blended. Add boiling water; stir vigorously until soft dough forms. Press dough in bottom and up side of pie plate, forming edge on rim of plate. Sprinkle bacon, cheese and onions over crust. In medium bowl, beat half-and-half, eggs, salt and red pepper with spoon until blended. Pour into crust. Bake 35 to 40 minutes or until edge is golden brown and center is set.

Cream Cheese Cinnamon Crescents

By: Aunt Paula
These are so yummy. Would be perfect for breakfast or
brunch or anytime! I just made a batch late this evening. A parent
brought these in for a teacher's luncheon and everyone loved them.

Ingredients

2 (8 ounce) cans crescent roll dough
2 (8 ounce) packages cream cheese
1 ¾ cups sugar
1 teaspoon vanilla
½ cup butter
1 teaspoon cinnamon

Directions

Roll out one can of crescent rolls in bottom of 9x13 pan sprayed with cooking spray. Cream together: 2 8oz. cream cheese, 1 cup sugar, 1 teaspoon vanilla. Spread this mixture over crescent rolls. Lay second tube of crescent rolls over mixture. Melt ½ cup butter, mix in ¾ cup sugar, 1 teaspoon cinnamon, and pour over top.

Bake at 350° for 30-35 minutes.

Welch Rarebit

Ree Drummond
Prep Time: 10 Minutes | Cook Time: 5 Minutes | Servings: 4

Ingredients

Slices Of Crusty Bread, Buttered And Browned Under The Broiler
2 Tablespoons Butter
2 Tablespoons Flour
$^1/_3$ cup Whole Milk
½ cup Beer
1 teaspoon (heaping) Dry Mustard
½ teaspoon Paprika
¼ teaspoon Cayenne
2 dashes Worcestershire
1-½ cup Sharp Cheddar Cheese, Grated
1 whole Egg Yolk
Fresh Chives, Chopped

Directions

Melt butter in a saucepan over low heat.

Sprinkle in flour and whisk together until combined. Cook over low heat for 2 minutes.

Pour in milk and beer, whisking constantly, and cook for an additional minute. Add mustard, paprika, and cayenne and whisk.

Add cheese and whisk slowly, cooking for a couple of minutes or until smooth, melted, and very hot.

Remove from heat and whisk in egg yolk,

Serve immediately (while hot) over toast. Sprinkle with chopped chives before serving.

Chicken with Lime Butter

Chicken breast halves, skinned and
boned
½ tsp. salt
½ tsp. pepper
$^1/_3$ cup oil
Juice of one lime
½ cup butter or margarine
½ tsp. minced chives
½ tsp. dill weed

Sprinkle chicken breasts on both sides with salt and pepper. In large
skillet heat oil then add chicken and sauté on one side until lightly
browned, about 4 minutes. Turn chicken and cover pan. Reduce heat
to low and cook 10 minutes or until tender. Remove from pan and
keep warm. Drain fat. Add lime juice to skillet and cook over low heat
until juice begins to bubble. Add butter and cook and stir until mixture
becomes opaque and thickened. Stir in chives and dill weed. Spoon
sauce over chicken.

Serves 6

Easy Feta Chicken Bake
Prep: 10 minutes Bake: 40 minutes
Makes 6 servings

Ingredients
6 boneless skinless chicken breast halves (about 2 lb.)
2 Tbsp. lemon juice, divided
¼ tsp. black pepper
1 pkg. (4 oz.) ATHENOS Traditional Crumbled Feta Cheese
¼ cup diced red pepper
¼ cup diced fresh parsley

Directions
PREHEAT oven to 350° F. Arrange chicken in 13x9-inch baking dish.
DRIZZLE with 1 tablespoon of the lemon juice. Season with black
pepper. Top with feta cheese; drizzle with remaining one tablespoon
of lemon juice. BAKE 35 to 40 minutes or until chicken cooked through.
Sprinkle with red pepper and parsley.

Chez Diana

Chicken Italiano

Ingredients

1 lb. of chicken, chopped
2 Tbsp. oil
1 can cheddar cheese soup
¼ cup chopped canned tomatoes
2 Tbsp. chopped onion
1 clove garlic
1 green pepper chopped
¼ tsp. oregano

Directions

In skillet, brown chicken in oil, drain off fat. Add remaining ingredients. Cover, simmer 45 minutes or until tender. Stir. Uncover for the last 5 minutes to thicken. Serve over rice or noodles.

Serves 4

Chicken and Mushrooms

From Suzanne Waddill

Ingredients

1 lb. fresh mushrooms, sliced
1 ½ lbs of chicken – cut up
1 lb. 4 oz. can unsweetened pineapple chunks (drained, save juice)
1 medium size green pepper, diced or sliced in rings
½ c. scallions, chopped
2 Tbsp. cornstarch
2 ½ tsp. salt
1 tsp. ground ginger

Directions

Broil chicken. Place chicken and pineapples, mushrooms, scallions, and green peppers in a 3 quart covered casserole dish. Mix pineapple juice, salt, ginger and cornstarch; pour over casserole. Cover and bake at 350 degrees for about 45 minutes. Serve over brown rice with cooked carrots as vegetable.

Chez Diana

Chicken Milano

Light and crunchy Italian-style chicken breasts partnered with a
salad can be on your dinner table in less than 30 minutes.
(Pictured here and on Salad Chapter Heading Page 39)

Dressing
1 tablespoon olive oil
2 teaspoons red wine vinegar
$^{1}/_{8}$ teaspoon salt

Salad
1 cup tightly packed arugula leaves
½ cup diced tomatoes
2 tablespoons diced red onion

Chicken
2 tablespoons Gold Medal® all-purpose flour
1 cup Progresso® Italian style panko crispy bread crumbs or Progresso®
   Italian style bread crumbs
1 egg
4 boneless skinless chicken breasts (about
1 ¼ lb)
2 tablespoons olive oil
¼ cup crumbled tomato-basil feta cheese

1. In medium bowl, mix dressing
   ingredients. Stir in salad ingredients
   to coat.

2. On separate plates, place flour and bread crumbs. In bowl, beat egg
   with fork. Coat chicken with flour. Dip into egg; coat well with bread
   crumbs.

3. In 12-inch nonstick skillet, heat 2 tablespoons oil over medium heat.
   Add chicken; cook 8 to 10 minutes, turning once, until juice of chicken
   is clear when center of thickest part is cut (170°F) and coating is golden
   brown. Serve chicken topped with salad and sprinkled with cheese.

Panko is the Japanese word for "bread crumbs." Unlike traditional bread
crumbs, panko is made from the soft, tender centers of bread instead of
the crust, which gives a light and crunchy texture.

Progresso® panko bread crumbs will stick best if you first shake the food in
flour, then dip into beaten egg before coating all sides with bread crumbs.

Makes: 4 servings

Chez Diana

Chicken Paprikash

From COOKS.COM

Ingredients

Boneless chicken breast (enough to serve each person)
½ stick butter
2 tbsp. garlic powder
3 tbsp. paprika
2 cans cream mushroom soup (I use 1)
8 oz. sour cream
16 oz. cooked egg noodles (medium)

Directions

Brown chicken in butter. Sprinkle with garlic and paprika. Add
mushroom soup and sour cream. Simmer until chicken is done.
Served over cooked egg noodles.

Mustard Crusted Chicken Breast

Prep time: 15 minutes Cook time: about 15 minutes

Ingredients

2 boneless, skinless chicken breasts
Garlic salt and freshly ground pepper to taste
¼ cup dijon mustard
1 tsp. tarragon
¾ cup panko bread crumbs (in the Asian foods section)
Oil for frying

Makes 2 servings.

Directions

Preheat oven to 425°F. Rinse chicken and pat dry. Pound with a meat
mallet between layers of plastic wrap to flatten slightly; lightly season
with garlic salt and pepper. Stir together mustard and tarragon and
spread on both sides of chicken. Dip into bread crumbs, pressing to coat
well. Heat ½ inch of oil in a medium ovenproof skillet until very hot.
Cook chicken for about 2 to 3 minutes per side or until golden brown.
Place skillet in oven and bake for 5 minutes more or until chicken is
cooked through.

Chez Diana

Hamptons Chicken Breasts

From California Wine Lover's Cookbook
Page 73

Ingredients

4 boned, skinless chicken breasts
4 Tbsp. butter
1 cup finely chopped onion
2 stalks of celery chopped
4 Tbsp. flour
1 cup white wine
1 cup chicken broth
1 cup milk
1 8-oz. package egg noodles, cooked and drained

Directions

Sauté chicken in butter for 2 minutes over medium heat. Cut breasts into
¾ inch chunks.
Add the onions and celery and sauté with chicken. Cover and cook 8 to
10 minutes.
Sprinkle flour over chicken, onion and celery mixture and stir well.
Add wine and chicken broth and stir well. Bring to a boil.
Add milk and simmer for 5 minutes.
Cook and drain egg noodles.
Serve chicken over egg noodles and garnish with fresh parsley.

Serves 4

Chez Diana

Oven-Fried Chicken Breasts

From Cook's Illustrated. Published July 15, 2008.

Although we like to use bone-in chicken for this recipe, you can substitute 4 boneless, skinless chicken breasts, and reduce the cooking time to 25 minutes. This recipe was printed in our cookbook The Best Light Recipe.

Ingredients

1 box plain Melba toast (about 5 ounces), broken into 1-inch pieces
2 tablespoons vegetable oil
3 large egg whites
1 tablespoon Dijon mustard
2 teaspoons minced fresh thyme leaves
¼ teaspoon garlic powder
$^1/_8$ teaspoon cayenne pepper
4 chicken breasts (about 10 ounces each)
Table salt and ground black pepper
Vegetable cooking spray

Directions

1. Adjust an oven rack to the upper-middle position and heat the oven to 450 degrees. Cover a baking sheet with foil and place a wire rack on top. Process the Melba toast into coarse crumbs in a food processor, about twelve 1-second pulses. Spread the crumbs in a shallow dish and toss with the oil.

2. In a separate shallow dish, whisk the egg whites, mustard, thyme, garlic powder, and cayenne together.

3. Pat the chicken dry with paper towels, then season with salt and pepper. Working with one piece of chicken at time, dip it into the egg white mixture, then coat with the Melba crumbs. Press on the Melba crumbs to make sure they adhere to the chicken. Lay the chicken on the wire rack and spray the tops with vegetable oil spray.

4. Bake until the coating is golden, the chicken is no longer pink in the center, and the thickest part registers 160 degrees on an instant read thermometer, about 40 minutes. Serve immediately.

Chez Diana

White Bean Chili

Prep Time: 20 min | Inactive Prep Time: 2 hr 0 min
Cook Time: 1 hr 45 min | Serves: 10 to 15 servings

Ingredients

1 pound dried navy beans
5 cups chicken stock
4 tablespoons (½ stick) butter
1 tablespoon minced garlic
¾ cup diced onion
1 ½ cups chopped green chilies (fresh or canned)
1 pound boneless, skinless chicken breasts, finely chopped
1 tablespoon ground cumin
1 tablespoon dried oregano
1 to 2 teaspoons ground black pepper
½ teaspoon white pepper
Pinch red pepper flakes
½ bunch cilantro leaves, chopped

Directions

Rinse beans well, cover with cool water, and soak for 2 hours.
Drain.
Place beans in large pot with chicken stock and bring to a boil over high heat. In a saucepan, heat butter over medium heat.
Add garlic, onion, and chilies and sauté for 5 minutes.
Add chile mixture to pot with beans.
Add chicken, cumin, oregano, pepper, white pepper, red pepper flakes, and cilantro.
Lower heat to medium and cook, stirring occasionally, for approximately 1 ½ hours.
Serve with cornbread, if desired.

Printed from FoodNetwork.com
on 09/25/2008
© 2008 Scripps Networks, LLC.
All Rights Reserved

Chez Diana

Rum Chicken

Yo, ho, ho and a chicken of rum. This tropical chicken dish is a taste of paradise. It's a real crowd pleaser for dinner parties, special events or any other occasion.

Ingredients

2 (8 oz.) cans sliced pineapple
1 (0.82 oz.) envelope commercial
  pina colada mix
¼ cup rum
¼ cup soy sauce
1 tsp. ground ginger
1 clove garlic, minced
8 chicken thighs, skinned
8 maraschino cherries

Ready in 2 hours

Directions

Drain pineapple, reserving juice; set pineapple aside. Combine pineapple juice, pina colada mix, rum, soy sauce, ginger and garlic. Place chicken in lightly greased 12 x 8 x 2-inch baking dish; add pineapple juice mixture. Marinate in refrigerator for 1 hour. Bake, uncovered, at 400 degrees for 30 minutes. Reduce heat to 350 degrees and bake for 20 minutes. Top with pineapple slices and maraschino cherries. Bake an additional 5 minutes.

Parmesan-Dijon Chicken

Perfectly seasoned and coated baked chicken breasts. Finally a way to wake up those boring weekday meals.

¼ cup butter or margarine, melted
2 tablespoons Dijon mustard
¾ cup Progresso® dry bread crumbs
  (any flavor)
¼ cup grated Parmesan cheese
6 boneless skinless chicken breast
  halves (1 ¾ pounds)

Heat oven to 375°F. Mix butter and mustard in shallow dish until well mixed. Mix bread crumbs and cheese in large plastic bag.

Dip one piece of chicken at a time into butter mixture, coating all sides. Then place in bag of bread crumbs,

seal bag and shake to coat with crumb mixture. Place chicken in single layer in ungreased rectangular pan, 13x9x2 inches.

Bake uncovered 20 to 30 minutes, turning once, until juice of chicken is no longer pink when centers of thickest pieces are cut.

Special Touch

Go ahead and add a pinch of this or a dash of that. Try adding dried basil, thyme, sage or rosemary leaves, dried dill weed or seasoned salt to taste to the bread crumb mixture.

Chez Diana

Turkey 'n Stuffing Bake

Submitted By: Earla Taylor

"Cooked turkey baked with stuffing, fried onions, peas and a creamy soup mixture. Great dish for those turkey leftovers!"

Ingredients

3 cups stuffing
1 (6 ounce) can French fried onions
1 (10.75 ounce) can condensed cream of celery soup
¾ cup milk
1 ½ cups cooked turkey, cubed
1 (10 ounce) package frozen green peas, thawed

Directions

1. Combine stuffing and 1/2 can onions. Spoon stuffing mixture into a 9 inch shallow baking dish. Press stuffing across bottom and up sides of dish to form a shell.

2. Combine undiluted soup, milk, turkey, and peas; pour into stuffing shell.

3. Bake, covered, at 350 degrees F (175 degrees C) for 30 minutes. Top with remaining onions. Bake, uncovered, 5 minutes longer. Serve hot.

Meats

Impossibly Easy Cheeseburger Pie

Get all the great taste of a cheeseburger magically baked in a pie.
Prep Time: 15 min | Start to Finish: 40 min

Ingredients

1 lb lean (at least 80%) ground beef
1 large onion, chopped (1 cup)
½ teaspoon salt
1 cup shredded Cheddar cheese (4 oz)
½ cup Original Bisquick® mix
1 cup milk
2 eggs

Makes: 6 servings

Heat oven to 400°F. Spray 9-inch glass pie plate with cooking spray. In 10-inch skillet, cook beef and onion over medium heat 8 to 10 minutes, stirring occasionally, until beef is brown; drain. Stir in salt. Spread in pie plate. Sprinkle with cheese. In small bowl, stir remaining ingredients with fork or wire whisk until blended. Pour into pie plate. Bake about 25 minutes or until knife inserted in center comes out clean.

Hamburger Diane

Ingredients

1 lb ground round
¾ tsp salt
⅛ tsp pepper
2 Tbsp butter
1 Tbsp prepared mustard
1 Tbsp lemon juice
½ Tbsp Worcestershire sauce

Directions

Mix the ground round, salt and pepper together lightly and form into 3 1-inch patties. Melt butter in skillet. Remove from heat. Blend mustard into butter, return to heat. Sauté hamburgers on medium heat about 5 minutes each side. Remove and keep warm. Add lemon juice and Worcestershire sauce to pan and stir over low heat until well blended. Return patties to pan and let simmer in juices a few minutes while spooning juice over the top occasionally.

Serves 2 or 3

Chez Diana

Corny Meat Loaf

From: 1986 Southern Living Annual Recipes

1 lb. ground beef
½ cup oatmeal
¼ cup diced onion
2 Tbsp. chopped parsley
½ cup frozen corn, thawed
2 Tbsp. salt-free herb and spice blend
1 ½ tsp. low sodium soy sauce
1 egg, beaten
2 Tbsp. low-fat yogurt
¼ cup plus 1 Tbsp. catsup, divided
Vegetable cooking spray

Directions

Combine ground beef, oats, onion, parsley, corn, herb-and-spice mix, and soy sauce in a mixing bowl; mix lightly. Combine egg and yogurt, add to meat mixture. Stir in ¼ cup ketchup. Shape into an 8 ½ X 4 ½ inch loaf. Place on a broiler pan sprayed with cooking spray. Bake, uncovered, at 350 degrees for 40 to 45 minutes. Spread remaining ketchup on top; bake an additional 5 minutes.

Yield: 6 servings.

Sloppy Joe (Mommy's recipe)

Ingredients

2 ½ lb hamburger
1 bottle catsup
4 T. Worcestershire sauce
4 T. vinegar
4 T. mustard
2 t. sugar
2 tsp. celery seed

Directions

In large skillet brown hamburger. Then add catsup, Worcestershire sauce, vinegar, prepared mustard, and sugar. Simmer several minutes. Add 2 teaspoons of celery seed. Serve in hamburger buns.

Chez Diana

Best-Ever Chili

1 ½ lbs ground beef
1 cup chopped onion
1 cup chopped green pepper
1 cup chopped celery
2 or 3 cans (15 oz.) chili or red
  kidney beans
2 (16-oz.) cans tomatoes, cut up
1 (6-oz.) can tomato paste
2 cloves garlic, crushed
1 ½ cup frozen corn
1-2 Tbsp. chili powder
2 tsp. salt
10 chopped jalapeno peppers

In Dutch oven cook beef, onion, green pepper, and celery until meat is brown and vegetables are tender. Drain.
Drain beans and add with all remaining ingredients.
Cover and simmer 1 to 1 ½ hour. I serve with macaroni and grated cheddar cheese.

Makes 5 servings

Hamburger Stroganoff

Popular ground beef version of the famous Russian meal.
From "Betty Crocker's New Picture Cookbook"

½ cup minced onion
1 clove garlic, minced
¼ cup butter
1 lb. ground beef
2 tbsp, flour
2 tsp, salt
¼ tsp. pepper
1 lb. fresh mushrooms or 1 can
  (8 oz.), sliced
1 can (10 ½ oz.) cream of
  chicken soup
1 cup commercial sour cream
2 tbsp, minced parsley
hot boiled noodles/spaghetti

Sauté onion and garlic in butter over medium heat. Add meat and brown. Add flour, salt, pepper and mushrooms. Cook 5 minutes. Add soup, simmer uncovered 10 minutes. Stir in sour cream. Heat through. Sprinkle with parsley. Serve with noodles.
4 to 6 servings

Chez Diana

Crustless Tex-Mex Meatloaf-Cheddar Pie

From Every Day with Rachael Ray May 2008
Prep Time: 20 min | Bake Time: 45 min
Serves 8

Turn meatloaf into an easy, cheesy pie.

Ingredients

One 16-ounce jar fire-roasted red peppers drained, split and seeded
12 ounces shredded Mexican cheese blend (3 cups)
1 ½ pounds lean ground beef
One 16-ounce jar chunky salsa
1 cup bread crumbs
2 eggs, lightly beaten
¹/₃ cup chopped flat-leaf parsley
¾ teaspoon salt
¾ teaspoon pepper

Directions

1. Preheat the oven to 375°. Grease a 10-inch pie plate lightly with olive oil and line with the red peppers. Scatter 1 cup cheese on top.

2. In a large bowl, mix 1 cup cheese, the beef, ¾ cup of the salsa, the bread crumbs, eggs, parsley, salt and pepper until just combined. Press into the pepper-and-cheese-lined pie plate. Spread the remaining salsa over the top. Bake for 35 minutes.

3. Scatter the remaining 1 cup cheese on top and bake for 10 minutes longer. Let cool for about 15 minutes before slicing.

Chez Diana

Creamed Dried Beef
With Artichokes

Yield: 4 servings | (Mrs. Harland J. Stone, Ocala, Florida)

Ingredients

1 tablespoon butter or margarine
1 (14-ounce) can artichoke hearts, drained and sliced
½ cup Chablis or other dry white wine
1 ½ tablespoons grated Parmesan cheese
1 (5-ounce) jar sliced dried beef, rinsed and coarsely chopped
1 (16-ounce) carton commercial sour cream
4 English muffins, halved and toasted
Paprika

Directions

Melt butter in a large skillet; add artichokes, Chablis, cheese, and dried beef, mixing well. Cook over medium heat, stirring often, until bubbly. Stir in sour cream; cook until thoroughly heated. (DO NOT BOIL) Serve over English muffin halves. Sprinkle with paprika.

Ham Loaf

From "What's Cookin?" Cookbook
Women's Society of Christian Service of the St. Paul's United Methodist Church
Red Lion, Pennsylvania Recipe of Mrs. Earl Lucius

Ingredients

1-½ lb. ham 1-½ lb. pork ground together
2 eggs
$^2/_3$ cup milk
1 cup bread crumbs
1 tbsp, mustard

Directions

Mix and make into a loaf. Bake 1 ½ hour at 350 degrees.
Baste every 15 minutes with the following:
1 cup brown sugar
2 tsps. dry mustard
½ cup vinegar
½ cup water

Chez Diana

Easy Pork Skillet

Prep Time: 10 min | Total Time: 20 min
Makes: 4 servings (about 1 cup each)
Pictured on Meat Chapter Heading Page 81.

Enjoy the flavors of pork, ramen noodles and fresh veggies in this done-in-a-flash stir-fry.

Ingredients

1 tablespoon vegetable oil
¾ pound pork tenderloin, cut into ¹/₈-inch strips
2 packages (3 ounces each) pork- flavored ramen noodles
1 ½ cups water
1 medium red bell pepper, cut into ¾ inch pieces (1 cup)
1 cup broccoli flowerets
4 medium green onions, cut into 1-inch pieces (½ cup)
1 tablespoon chopped fresh parsley or 2 teaspoons parsley flakes,
 if desired
1 tablespoon soy sauce

Directions

1. Heat 12-inch skillet or wok over medium-high heat. Add oil; rotate skillet to coat side.

2. Add pork; stir-fry about 5 minutes or until pork is no longer pink.

3. Gently break apart noodles. Stir noodles, seasonings from flavor packets and remaining ingredients into pork. Heat to boiling. Boil 3 to 4 minutes, stirring occasionally, until noodles are completely softened.

This is the perfect place to use a bag of chopped broccoli flowerets. Or buy broccoli flowerets from the salad bar section of your supermarket. Play with the colors in this ten-minute recipe. Use cauliflower instead of broccoli and green or yellow bell peppers instead of red.

Nutrition Information: 1 Serving: Calories 345 (Calories from Fat 135); Total Fat 15 g (Saturated Fat 4 g); Cholesterol 55 mg; Sodium 980 mg; Total Carbohydrate 30 g (Dietary Fiber 3 g); Protein 25 g Percent Daily Value*: Vitamin A 50 %; Vitamin C 54 %; Calcium 4 %; Iron 14 % Exchanges: 2 Starch; 3 Lean Meat; ½ Fat *Percent Daily Values are based on a 2,000 calorie diet.

Chez Diana

Baked Pork with Sauerkraut

Recipes on Parade Foreign Foods
Mrs. L. M. Cuchna, Parlm. OCWC
Granite City Army Depot, Illinois

6 lean pork chops
2 Tbsp. flour
1 Tbsp. shortening
1 1-lb. can sauerkraut, drained and rinsed
½ tsp. caraway seed
1 medium apple, sliced thin
1 can cream of mushroom soup
Salt and pepper to taste

Dust chops with flour; brown in shortening. Combine sauerkraut, caraway seed, apple, soup, salt and pepper; blend together. Place chops on sauerkraut; cover. Bake at 400 degrees for 15 minutes. Reduce heat to 350 degrees and bake for 1 hour and 30 minutes.

Yield: 3 servings

Pork Chops In Wine Sauce

From "Cooking In Style" Cookbook By Charlotte Adams

4 loin pork chops, 1 inch thick
2 tablespoons butter
I small onion, chopped
1 tablespoon flour
½ cup dry white wine
¼ cup beef stock
1 tsp. Dijon mustard
2 tsp. capers
Salt and Freshly Ground Pepper

Brown chops in butter over medium heat for about 20 minutes on each side. Remove chops. Add onion and brown slowly. Blend in flour. Add wine and stock and stir constantly until mixture thickens. Return chops to sauce and simmer 10 minutes. Add mustard and capers and season to taste, mixing well.

Serves 4.

Chez Diana

Italian Sausages, Potatoes & Artichoke Hearts in Tomato Broth

Active Time: 20 Minutes | Total Time: 50 Minutes

Simmering chunks of potato, Italian sausages, and artichoke hearts in a tomato broth melds their flavors into a savory stew. From Food and Wine Magazine.

Ingredients

1 tablespoon olive oil
1 ½ pounds mild Italian sausages
3 cloves garlic, cut into thin slices
1 ½ pounds boiling potatoes (about 5), cut into 1-inch chunks
½ teaspoon dried thyme
¹/₃ cup dry white wine
1 ¼ cups canned low-sodium chicken broth or homemade stock
1 cup canned crushed tomatoes in thick puree
1 ½ cups drained and rinsed halved canned artichoke hearts (one 14-ounce can)
6 tablespoons chopped fresh parsley
½ teaspoon salt
½ teaspoon fresh-ground black pepper

Directions

In a large stainless-steel pot, heat the oil over moderately high heat. Add the sausages and brown well, about 10 minutes. Remove. Pour off all but 1 tablespoon of the fat.

Reduce the heat to moderate. Add the garlic, potatoes, and thyme. Cook, stirring occasionally, until the potatoes are lightly browned, about 5 minutes. Add the wine and boil until reduced to approximately 3 tablespoons, 2 to 3 minutes. Stir in the broth, tomatoes, artichoke hearts, 4 tablespoons of the parsley, the salt, and the sausages.

Bring to a simmer and cook, partially covered, until the potatoes are tender, about 30 minutes. Add the remaining 2 tablespoons parsley and the pepper.

Substitute: Rosemary for the thyme
Red wine for the white wine
Hot Italian sausage for the mild

Chez Diana

Jambalaya

Ingredients

1 tablespoon olive oil, separated
1 small onion, chopped
½ cup celery, chopped
1 green (I use red) pepper, chopped
1 garlic clove, minced
1 14.5 oz. can chopped tomatoes, drained
2 Tbsp. tomato paste
1 Tbsp. parsley
1 tsp. Tabasco sauce
1 tsp. salt
½ cup water
1 ½ cup pinto beans, rinsed & drained
8 oz. sausage links, cut into 1 inch pieces
4-5 cups hot cooked long grain brown rice

Directions

Cook the sausage in 1 ½ tsp. oil until browned, about 5 minutes, and set aside. In large pot, heat remaining 1 ½ tsp. olive oil over medium heat. Add onion, celery, & bell pepper and sauté for 5 minutes, or until the vegetables begin to soften. Add garlic, tomatoes, tomato paste, Tabasco sauce, parsley, salt and water. Cover and simmer for 20 minutes, or until vegetables are soft. Add the beans. Add cooked sausage to the tomato mixture and simmer for about 10 minutes, until flavors are well blended. Adjust the seasonings. Serve over the hot cooked rice.

Seafood

Easy Salmon Cakes

Source: © EatingWell Magazine
4 servings

Ingredients

3 teaspoons extra-virgin olive oil, divided
1 small onion, finely chopped
1 stalk celery, finely diced
2 tablespoons chopped fresh parsley
15 ounces canned salmon, drained, or 1 ½ cups cooked salmon
1 large egg, lightly beaten
1 ½ teaspoons Dijon mustard
1 ¾ cups fresh whole-wheat breadcrumbs
½ teaspoon freshly ground pepper
Creamy Dill Sauce (See recipe below)
1 lemon, cut into wedges

Directions

Preheat oven to 450 degrees F. Coat a baking sheet with cooking spray.
Heat 1 ½ teaspoons oil in a large nonstick skillet over medium-high heat.

Add onion and celery; cook, stirring, until softened, about 3 minutes. Stir in parsley; remove from the heat.
Place salmon in a medium bowl. Flake apart with a fork; remove any bones and skin. Add egg and mustard; mix well. Add the onion mixture, breadcrumbs and pepper; mix well. Shape the mixture into 8 patties, about 2 ½ inches wide.
Heat remaining 1 ½ teaspoons oil in the pan over medium heat. Add 4 patties and cook until the undersides are golden, 2 to 3 minutes. Using a wide spatula, turn them over onto the prepared baking sheet. Repeat with the remaining patties. Cook the salmon cakes until golden on top and heated through, 15 to 20 minutes. Meanwhile, prepare Creamy Dill Sauce. Serve salmon cakes with sauce and lemon wedges.

Creamy Dill Sauce

Ingredients

¼ cup reduced-fat mayonnaise
¼ cup nonfat plain yogurt
2 scallions, thinly sliced
1 tablespoon lemon juice
1 tablespoon chopped fresh dill/parsley
Freshly ground pepper to taste

Directions

Combine mayonnaise, yogurt, scallions, lemon juice, dill (or parsley) and pepper in a small bowl and mix well.

Chez Diana

Broiled Salmon Steaks with Herb Sauce

From "Seafood Moods" Cookbook
Pictured on Seafood Chapter Heading Page

Ingredients

Salmon steaks or salmon
¼ cup butter or margarine
¼ cup white wine
1 tablespoon chopped parsley
¼ tsp. fines herbes blend
1 clove garlic, minced
1 tsp. salt

Directions

In an ovenproof pan, combine butter or margarine, wine parsley, herbs and garlic; heat slowly until butter is melted (I use microwave). Place fish in sauce and broil about 3 inches from heat source, 4 to 6 minutes. Turn fish carefully and broil 4 to 6 minutes until fish flakes easily when tested with a fork.

Sole with Mushroom-Wine Sauce

From "Seafood Moods" Cookbook

Ingredients

2 lbs sole fillets
3 Tbsp. butter or margarine, separated
2 Tbsp. lemon juice
1 ⅛ tsp. salt
2 slices bacon, cooked, drained, & crumbled
¼ cup green onions, chopped
1 clove garlic, minced
½ cup fresh or canned drained mushrooms
1 tsp. flour
¼ cup catsup
¼ cup dry white wine
¼ cup water

Directions

Arrange fish in single layer in well buttered baking pan. Drizzle 2 Tbsp. melted butter and lemon juice over fish and sprinkle with salt. Broil 4 inches from heat source for about 10 minutes or until fish flakes when tested with a fork. While fish is broiling, fry bacon until crisp, drain and crumble. Add 1 Tbsp. butter to bacon drippings. Cook green onions and garlic in drippings until tender. Stir in mushrooms and flour. Add catsup, wine, water and ⅛ tsp. salt. Cook, stirring constantly until sauce is thickened. Spoon sauce over fish, sprinkle with bacon pieces.
Serves 6

Chez Diana

Sesame Sole

From "Reader's Digest Great Recipes for Good Health" Cookbook

Ingredients

¼ cup buttermilk
4 sole, flounder, or other white fish
 fillets (about 5 ounces each)
2 tsp. Dijon mustard
2 tsp. low-sodium tomato paste
½ tsp. dried tarragon
2 Tbsp. flour
3 ½ Tbsp. sesame seeds
4 tsp. vegetable oil
Lemon slices for serving

Pour buttermilk in a shallow dish and dip the fillets in it, coating well all over. Lay the fillets on a platter. Combine the mustard, tomato paste and tarragon, and spread on both sides of the fillets. Combine flour and sesame seeds and press the fillets into the mixture to coat all over. Place on a rack and refrigerate, uncovered for 30 minutes, to make the coating stick. In a 12-inch skillet, heat vegetable oil over medium heat and cook fish fillets until golden – about 1 ½ minutes on each side. Garnish with lemon slices to serve.

Sauteed Tilapia Fillets With Lime

25 min | 15 min prep
We also use different kinds of fish: cod, sole, catfish, orange roughy & flounder.

1-1 ⅓ lb tilapia fillet, about ½ inch
 thick
3 tablespoons all-purpose flour
salt and pepper
1 clove garlic, minced or pressed
½ cup dry white wine
1 tablespoon lime juice
½ tablespoon butter
1 tablespoon olive oil
3 green onions, chopped

Directions

Rinse the fish and pat dry. Put the flour on a plate and season it with salt and pepper. Dredge fillets in the flour, patting to remove excess. In a small bowl, combine the garlic, wine, lime juice and butter, & set aside. Heat the oil in a 10 to 12-inch frying pan over medium-high heat. Add the fillets without overlapping (you may need to cook in 2 batches). Cook until golden on the bottom, about 3 minutes. Turn fillets over & cook until opaque through the thickest part, 1 to 2 minutes more. Transfer the fish to a platter & keep warm (cover with foil or place in a 200 degree oven). Add the wine mixture to pan and boil, scraping up cooked bits, until reduced by half, 2 to 3 minutes. Stir in the onions and heat on low about 30 seconds. Pour the sauce over the fish & serve.
Serves 4

Chez Diana

Sautéed Tilapia with White Wine & Lemon Sauce

This is one of my new favorites. I love the lemon sauce over the Tilapia—perfect for anytime of the year. You can use other white flesh fish as well.

Sautéed Tilapia

½ Cup flour
3 tablespoons olive oil
4 Tilapia Fillets — fresh
Kosher salt and pepper — to taste

Place flour in shallow baking dish or pie plate and set aside. Pat fish fillets with a paper towel, season both sides of fillet with salt and pepper and let stand until fillets are glistening with moisture, about 5 minutes. If you going to make the White Wine Sauce — do it now while the fish is resting. (Follow the directions for the sauce) Coat the Fish: Coat both sides of fillet with flour and shake off excess and place them on a separate plate or paper towel, preferably in one single layer.

Sauté the Fish: Heat 2 Tablespoons of the olive oil over high heat in a large non-stick skillet until oil is shimmering, but not smoking. Place the fillets in a single layer and immediately reduce heat to medium-high. ** Depending on the size of your skillet and the amount of fish you're making, you'll have to add more oil and sauté the fillets in batches. Without moving the fish, sauté for 2 to 3 minutes on each side and until the edges of fillet are opaque and bottoms are lightly browned. Use the spatula to gently flip fillets. Transfer fillets onto plate and if you're using the sauce, pour it over now and serve.

Serving Size: 4

White Wine and Lemon Sauce

1 tablespoon olive oil
1 shallot (other onion can be substituted in a pinch) — roughly chopped
½ cup white wine
2 tablespoons butter
1 tablespoon fresh parsley
½ lemon

In a sauce pan, heat 1 tablespoon of the olive oil over medium heat. Sauté shallots until softened and beginning to color, about 1 ½ minutes. Add wine, increase heat to high and bring to boil, boil until reduced to ¼ cup — about 3-5 minutes. Remove sauce pan from burner and pour into another container, such as a coffee mug or creamer, through a small strainer to strain out the shallot, and then discard the shallot. Whisk in butter and parsley — and a squeeze of half a lemon. Set aside and keep warm until the fish is done.

Chez Diana

Creamy Curried Tuna

From "Seafood Moods" Cookbook

1 cup chopped celery
¼ cup diced green pepper
2 Tbsp. butter or margarine
1 can (10 ½ oz.) condensed cream
  of chicken soup
²/₃ cup milk
¼ cup salad dressing/mayonnaise
1 tsp. curry powder
½ tsp. salt
2 cans (6 ½ to 7 oz. each) tuna,
  drained
¼ cup diced pimiento
Rice or patty shells

Directions

Sauté celery and green pepper in butter or margarine until vegetables are tender. Add soup, milk, salad dressing/mayonnaise, curry powder, and salt. Mix well and heat slowly, stirring constantly. Fold in tuna and pimiento; heat to serving temperature. Serve on rice or in patty shells.

Makes 4-6 servings

Deviled Tuna Pot Pie

From "Reader's Digest Great Recipes for Good Health" Cookbook

1 Tbsp. margarine
1 small onion, chopped
2 stalks of celery, chopped
2 cloves garlic, minced
1 cup frozen corn
1 jar pimientos, drained
4 tsp. flour
1 cup low sodium chicken broth
½ cup skim milk
2 Tbsp. Parmesan cheese
2 Tbsp. Dijon mustard
2 tsp. lemon juice
2 cans tuna (6 oz. each) drained
Refrigerator biscuits
Paprika

Preheat oven to 450 degrees. In medium saucepan melt margarine, add onion, garlic, corn, pimientos, and pepper. Cover and cook for 5 minutes until onion is soft. Blend in the flour, then add chicken broth and milk stirring constantly until thickened. Add parmesan cheese and mustard and lemon juice. Remove from heat and fold in the tuna. Transfer to an ungreased 5 or 6 cup oven proof casserole. Arrange the biscuits on top and sprinkle with paprika. Bake uncovered, for 15 minutes, until biscuits are golden.
Serves 4

Chez Diana

Country Dijon Tuna Pasta Casserole/Salad

Ingredients

1 pound elbow or any round-shaped pasta, cooked according to
  package directions
1 cup non-fat plain yogurt
¼ cup whole grain Dijon-style mustard
1 cup diced celery
½ cup diced green bell pepper
½ cup diced red bell pepper
½ cup diced red onion
1 (12-oz.) can Chicken of the Sea Solid White Albacore Tuna in
  Spring Water
Garlic salt and pepper

Directions

Drain and rinse pasta in cold water; set aside. In a large bowl, mix yogurt
and mustard until well blended. Add celery, bell peppers, onion and
pasta into dressing mixture; blend well. Gently fold in Chicken of the Sea
Tuna. Add garlic salt and pepper to taste if necessary. Serve immediately
OR chill until ready to serve. Makes 10 servings.

Preparation Time: 20 minutes

Aunt Irene's Tuna Loaf

From John's Aunt Irene Farina

Ingredients

2 cans of tuna, drained (about 9 or
10 oz. total)
2 oz. Parmesan cheese
2 oz. bread crumbs
2 eggs
Pinch of salt, optional
Chopped parsley

Drain tuna well and separate/ mash. Add parmesan cheese, bread crumbs, parsley and eggs. Mix well with wooden spoon. Wrap in saran wrap, then double wrap in plastic bags – tie off well. Heat 2 quarts of water in pot to boiling. Add wrapped tuna loaf. Boil for 30 minutes. Immediately remove plastic bags and saran wrap and slice to serve.

Chez Diana

Orange Sauced Roughy

(Pictured)

4 to 5 orange roughy fillets
½ cup fresh orange juice
2 tsp. cornstarch
⅓ cup chicken broth or dry white wine
1 tsp. sugar
¼ tsp. dried thyme leaves
1 tsp. vegetable oil

OVEN DIRECTIONS: Combine juice, broth (or wine), cornstarch, sugar and thyme in 1 quart saucepan. Cook over medium heat until sauce boils or is thickened and translucent, stirring constantly. Set aside. Spray large baking sheet with nonstick vegetable cooking spray. Arrange fillets on baking sheet and brush evenly with oil. Place fillets 6 inches from the heat and broil for 4 to 5 minutes or until the fish is firm & opaque and begins to flake. Top with sauce.

MICROWAVE DIRECTIONS: Combine juice, broth (or wine), cornstarch, sugar and thyme in microwaveable bowl. Microwave on high for 3 to 4 minutes. Set aside. Arrange fillets on microwaveable dish. Microwave on high for 2 minutes. Rotate and microwave for 2 minutes or until fish flakes easily with a fork. Top with sauce.

Pasta/Rice Dishes

Chez Diana

Skillet Lasagna

The Washington Post, January 4, 2006
Lasagna is usually too labor-intensive to bother with during the week.
With this version, though, you can sit down to dinner after just the
time it would normally take to bake the lasagna. Being made on the
stovetop, this version is not layered; instead, it substitutes farfalle for the
customary long, flat pasta. But all the traditional flavors tomato-based sauce,
meat and three cheeses in addition to the pasta are still here. Italian
sausage is robust, but turkey sausage makes an acceptable substitute.

Ingredients

8 ounces flat, dried pasta
$^1/_3$ pound Italian sausage or turkey sausage (sweet or hot)
½ cup finely chopped onion
½ cup chopped green bell pepper
1 small zucchini, diced
2 cloves garlic, minced
1 can (14.5 ounces) no-salt-added tomato sauce
2 teaspoons dried oregano
½ teaspoon dried basil
¼ teaspoon dried thyme
Salt & Freshly ground black pepper
½ cup part-skim ricotta cheese
¼ cup (1 ounce) part-skim mozzarella cheese, grated
2 tablespoons grated Parmesan cheese
2 tablespoons chopped flat-leaf parsley
1 large egg, lightly beaten

In a large pot of boiling salted water, cook the pasta until it is just barely
done and still firm; do not overcook. Drain and set aside.
Meanwhile, in a large skillet over medium-high heat, brown the sausage,
breaking up the clumps with a spoon, about 3 minutes. Add the onion
and bell pepper and cook, stirring, for 3 minutes. Add the zucchini and
garlic and cook for 1 minute. Drain off the fat. Stir in the tomato sauce,
oregano, basil and thyme and salt and pepper to taste. Reduce the heat
to medium and cook for 10 minutes. In a medium bowl, mix the three
cheeses, parsley, egg and more black
pepper to taste. Add the cheese mixture and the pasta to the skillet.
Cover and cook over medium-low heat for 15 minutes, stirring
occasionally. Let stand for 5 minutes before serving.

4 servings

Chez Diana

Spaghetti with Creamy Clam Sauce

This creamy version of the ever-popular pasta with clam sauce
cooks in minutes. If small cans of minced clams are pantry staples,
you can prepare an enticing meal with very little notice. Serve with a
green salad and crusty bread to soak up the sauce.

Ingredients

8 ounces dried spaghetti or linguine or 1 pound fresh linguine or other ribbon pasta

For Sauce:
2 6-½ ounce cans minced clams
Half and half, light cream, or milk
½ cup chopped onion
2 cloves garlic, minced
2 tablespoons margarine or butter
¼ cup all-purpose flour
½ teaspoon dried basil or
oregano, crushed
¼ teaspoon salt
¼ teaspoon pepper
¼ cup snipped fresh parsley
¼ cup dry white wine
¼ cup grated parmesan cheese

Directions

In a large saucepan or pasta pot bring 3 quarts water to boiling. Add pasta. Reduce heat slightly. Boil, uncovered, for 8-12 minutes for dried pasta or 1 ½-2 minutes for fresh, or till al dente, stirring occasionally. (Or, cook according to package directions.) Immediately drain.

FOR SAUCE: Meanwhile, drain clams, reserving liquid. Add enough half-and-half, light cream, or milk to the reserved liquid to make 1 and ¾ cups. In a medium saucepan cook the onion and garlic in hot margarine or butter for about 5 minutes, or till onion is tender but not brown. Stir in the flour, basil or oregano, salt, and pepper. Add the cream mixture all at once. Cook and stir till thickened and bubbly. Cook and stir for 1 minute more. Stir in the parsley, wine, and clams. Heat through. Serve sauce over hot pasta. Sprinkle with Parmesan cheese. Serve immediately.

Yield: Makes 4 main-dish servings

Chez Diana

Penne alla Vodka

From the Episode: Pasta and Tomatoes, Reimagined
So that the sauce and pasta finish cooking at the same time, drop the
pasta into boiling water just after adding the vodka to the sauce. If possible,
use premium vodka; inexpensive brands will taste harsh in this sauce.
Pepper vodka imparts a pleasant flavor and can be substituted for plain.

1 (28 ounce) can whole tomatoes,
 drained, liquid reserved
2 tablespoons olive oil
½ small onion, minced (about ¼ cup)
1 tablespoon tomato paste
2 medium cloves garlic, minced
 or pressed through garlic press
 (about 2 teaspoons)

¼-½ teaspoon hot red pepper
 flakes
Table salt
⅓ cup vodka
½ cup heavy cream
1 pound penne pasta
2 tablespoons minced fresh basil
 leaves
Grated Parmesan cheese, for serving

1. Puree half of tomatoes in
 food processor until smooth.
 Dice remaining tomatoes into
 ½-inch pieces, discarding cores.
 Combine pureed and diced
 tomatoes in liquid measuring
 cup (you should have about 1
 ⅔ cups). Add reserved liquid to
 equal 2 cups.
2. Heat oil in large saucepan over
 medium heat until shimmering.
 Add onion and tomato paste
 and cook, stirring occasionally,
 until onions are light golden
 around edges, about 3 minutes.
 Add garlic and pepper flakes;
 cook, stirring constantly, until
 fragrant, about 30 seconds.
3. Stir in tomatoes and ½ teaspoon
 salt. Remove pan from heat
 and add vodka. Return pan to
 medium-high heat and simmer
 briskly until alcohol flavor is
 cooked off, 8 to 10 minutes; stir
 frequently and lower heat to

medium if simmering becomes
too vigorous. Stir in cream and
cook until hot, about 1 minute.
4. Meanwhile, bring 4 quarts water
 to boil in large Dutch oven over
 high heat. Add 1 tablespoon
 salt and pasta. Cook until just
 shy of al dente, then drain
 pasta, reserving ¼ cup cooking
 water, and transfer pasta back
 to Dutch oven. Add sauce to
 pasta and toss over medium
 heat until pasta absorbs some
 of sauce, 1 to 2 minutes, and
 adding reserved cooking water
 if sauce is too thick. Stir in basil
 and adjust seasoning with salt.
 Divide among pasta bowls and
 serve immediately, passing
 Parmesan separately.

Serves 4

Chez Diana

Pasta With Tomato Sauce With Chickpeas

From "NO-COOK PASTA SAUCES "Cookbook
Earthy and rustic, I find the combination of tomatoes and chickpeas
deeply satisfying indeed. Try adding crumbled feta cheese, Gaeta olives,
and green onions if you fancy a more potent pasta.

3 tablespoons fruity olive oil
2 large garlic cloves, finely chopped
¼ teaspoon crushed red pepper, or to taste
1 lb. fresh, ripe tomatoes, seeded & coarsely diced
1 can (19 ounces) chickpeas, rinsed and well drained
½ teaspoon dried oregano
½ teaspoon salt, or to taste
Freshly ground black pepper ¼ cup freshly grated Pecorino
  Romano cheese, plus extra for serving
¼ cup fresh flat-leaf parsley, coarsely chopped
¼ cup fresh basil leaves, coarsely chopped

Combine olive oil, garlic, crushed red pepper, tomatoes, chickpeas,
oregano, salt, pepper, and Romano cheese in pasta serving bowl. Set
aside to warm to room temperature or, preferably, place the bowl (be
sure it's heatproof) over the pasta pot to warm the ingredients while
heating the water. Once the water comes to a boil, remove bowl and set
aside. Cook pasta in large pot of boiling salted water until al dente. Drain
pasta well and immediately add to sauce in bowl. Sprinkle with parsley
and basil and toss. Serve at once with extra Romano cheese.

Serves 2 to 4

Chez Diana

Macaroni with Chickpeas & Tomatoes

From Reader's Digest "Great Recipes for Good Health" Cookbook
Preparation: 5 minutes | Cooking time: 24 minutes

Ingredients

1 Tbsp. olive oil
1 clove garlic, minced
1 can (1 lb.) tomatoes, chopped
  with juice
2 Tbsp. chopped parsley
½ tsp. each basil and oregano
¼ tsp. black pepper
1 cup cooked and drained chickpeas
8 oz. cooked macaroni

Serves 4

Directions

Heat olive oil in medium sized pan over moderate heat; add garlic and cook for 30 seconds. Mix in the tomatoes, parsley, basil, oregano and pepper; bring to a boil, lower the heat so mixture bubbles and simmer uncovered for 10 minutes. Stir in the chickpeas and cook 10 minutes longer. Meanwhile, cook the macaroni, drain well and transfer to serving bowl. Pour chickpea mixture over all and serve.

Noodles Austin

From "Cooking With Style" by Charlotte Adams

Ingredients

8 oz. fine noodles
1 cup cottage cheese
2 cups sour cream
1 clove garlic, minced
1 onion finely chopped
1 Tbsp. Worcestershire sauce
Dash Tabasco sauce
Salt to taste
Parmesan Cheese

Serves 4-6

Directions

Cook noodles in boiling salted water for nine minutes. Drain well. Mix with cottage cheese, 1 cup of sour cream, garlic, onion, Worcestershire sauce, Tabasco, and salt. Spoon into a buttered casserole. Bake in 350 degree oven for 45 minutes or until brown and crusty on top. Serve with remaining sour cream and Parmesan on the side, so guests may top their noodles as they are served.

Chez Diana

Penne Putanesca

From "Controlling Your Fat Tooth" Cookbook
By Joseph Piscatella

1 Tbsp. olive oil
1 cup chopped onion
5 cloves garlic, minced
1 28-oz. can canned tomatoes
  chopped
½ tsp. crushed red pepper
½ tsp. salt
1 c. olive, chopped
4 anchovies, chopped
1 jar drained capers
1 lb. penne pasta, cooked and
  drained
$^1/_3$ cup Parmesan

In a non-stick skillet, heat olive oil. Add onions and garlic, and sauté 6-8 minutes. Add tomatoes, red peppers and salt. Heat to boiling, reduce heat and simmer 10 minutes. Add olives, anchovies and capers.

Serve over cooked drained pasta. Sprinkle with Parmesan.

Serves 6-8

Pasta Primavera

Recipe courtesy of Giada de Laurentiis

Ingredients

3 carrots, peeled and cut into thin
  strips
2 medium zucchini or 1 large
  zucchini, cut into thin strips
2 yellow squash, cut into thin strips
1 onion, thinly sliced
1 yellow bell pepper, cut into thin
  strips
1 red bell pepper, cut into thin
  strips
¼ cup olive oil
Kosher salt and freshly ground
  black pepper
1 tablespoon dried Italian herbs or
  herbes de Provence
1 pound farfalle (bowtie pasta)
15 cherry tomatoes, halved
½ cup grated Parmesan

Serves 6

Preheat the oven to 450 degrees F. On a large heavy baking sheet, toss all of the vegetables with the oil, salt, pepper, and dried herbs to coat. Bake until the carrots are tender and the vegetables begin to brown, stirring after the first 10 minutes, about 20 minutes total. Meanwhile, cook the pasta in a large pot of boiling salted water until al dente, tender but still firm to the bite, about 8 minutes. Drain, reserving 1 cup of the cooking liquid. Toss the pasta with the vegetable mixtures in a large bowl to combine. Toss with cherry tomatoes & enough reserved cooking liquid to moisten. Season the pasta with salt and pepper, to taste. Sprinkle with the Parmesan and serve immediately.

Chez Diana

Lone Star Steak and Pasta

Ingredients

1 pound rotini pasta
1 ¼ pounds top sirloin steak — boneless, 1" thick
1 tablespoon olive oil
¼ cup lime juice
10 ounces canned tomatoes with green chiles — undrained
16 ounces black beans, canned — rinsed and drained (I use pinto beans)
1 cup green pepper — chopped
1 cup frozen corn — thawed and drained
¼ cup green onion — sliced
½ cup cilantro leaves, whole — loosely packed
2 teaspoons garlic — minced
½ teaspoon ground cumin
1 teaspoon salt

Directions

Cook pasta according to package directions. While pasta is cooking, trim the fat from the steak and cut lengthwise in half and then crosswise into $^1/_8$ " thick strips.

Heat oil in a large nonstick skillet over medium-high heat. Add steak, half at a time, and cook 1 to 2 minutes or until the outside surface is no longer pink. Remove steak and set aside.

In the same skillet, add lime juice, tomatoes and chiles, black beans, green pepper, corn, onion, cilantro, garlic, cumin and salt. Cook and stir until hot. Add the cooked steak and cook until heated through.

Serve over pasta.

Serving Size: 6

Chez Diana

Three-Cheese Manicotti

Prep: 50 minutes | Bake: 35 minutes

Ingredients

¼ cup chopped onion
1 clove garlic, minced
1 tablespoon cooking oil
1 14-½-ounce can tomatoes, cut up
1 8-ounce can tomato sauce
1 teaspoon sugar
1 teaspoon dried oregano, crushed
¼ teaspoon dried thyme, crushed
1 small bay leaf
8 dried manicotti shells

2 beaten eggs
2 cups shredded mozzarella cheese (8 ounces)
1-½ cups ricotta cheese or cream-style cottage cheese
½ cup grated Parmesan cheese
½ cup snipped fresh parsley
½ teaspoon dried oregano, crushed
Dash pepper

Directions

1. For sauce, in a 2-quart saucepan cook onion and garlic in hot oil until tender. Add undrained tomatoes, tomato sauce, sugar, the 1 teaspoon oregano, the thyme, and bay leaf. Bring to boiling; reduce heat. Simmer, uncovered, for 20 to 25 minutes or until thickened. Remove from heat; discard bay leaf.
2. Meanwhile, cook pasta according to package directions; drain. Rinse shells in cold water.
3. For filling, in a medium mixing bowl stir together eggs, half of the mozzarella cheese, the ricotta or cottage cheese, Parmesan cheese, parsley, the ½ teaspoon oregano, and dash pepper. Spoon filling into manicotti.
4. Pour half of the tomato mixture into a 2-quart rectangular baking dish. Arrange stuffed manicotti in the baking dish. Pour remaining sauce over shells. Sprinkle remaining mozzarella cheese atop.
5. Bake the stuffed manicotti, covered, in a 350 degree F oven for 35 to 40 minutes or until heated through.

Makes 8 servings

Make-Ahead Tip: Prepare as above, except do not bake.
Cover and chill in the refrigerator for up to 24 hours. Bake as above.

Light and Creamy Mac and Cheese

Six ingredients and ten minutes create a one-dish mac and cheese just for two.
Prep Time: 10 min | Total Time: 10 min

1 cup uncooked jumbo elbow macaroni (3 oz)
$^1/_3$ cup Green Giant® Valley Fresh Steamers™ frozen sweet peas
$^2/_3$ cup fat-free (skim) milk
1 oz reduced-fat cream cheese (Neufchatel), cut into small pieces, softened
2 slices (¾ oz each) American cheese
2 tablespoons crushed fat-free herb-seasoned croutons

Cook and drain macaroni as directed on package, omitting salt and adding peas for the last 5 minutes of cooking. Meanwhile, in 10-inch nonstick skillet, heat milk, cream cheese and American cheese over medium-low heat, stirring carefully with wire whisk, until cheese is melted. Using a wire whisk will help make it easier to stir the cream cheese into the milk. Add cooked macaroni and peas to cheese sauce; stir to coat. Let stand 2 to 3 minutes or until slightly thickened. Serve topped with croutons.

Makes: 2 servings

Low Fat Macaroni and Cheese

Ingredients

1 cup fat-free milk
1 ¼ cups shredded reduced-fat Cheddar cheese
$^2/_3$ cup fat-free cottage cheese
pepper to taste
2 ½ cups cooked elbow macaroni
1 tbsp. grated onion
Paprika

Directions

In a blender combine the milk, cheeses and pepper. Cover and process until creamy. Pour into a bowl; stir in macaroni and onion. Transfer to a 1-½-qt. baking dish coated with nonstick cooking spray. Sprinkle with paprika and bake, uncovered, at 350 degrees for 1 hour or until heated through.

Chez Diana

Pasta with Hot Dogs

From Woman's Day Magazine of June 23, 1998

1 pound pasta cooked & drained
15-oz. can black or pinto beans
1 cup corn (I use frozen – thawed)
1 cup chopped green pepper
½ cup chopped onion
4 hot dogs

For dressing:
$^1/_3$ cup barbeque sauce
3 Tbsp. vinegar
½ cup mayonnaise
1 tsp. salt

Cook hot dogs in microwave.
Mix pasta and rest of ingredients including hot dogs.
Mix dressing ingredients and add to pasta.
May be served hot or chill and serve as a pasta salad.

Serves 4

Spinach, Tomato and Olive Pasta

I was a little worried about this recipe because I'm not a huge fan of cooked spinach but the feta drew me in so we went with it. IT WAS AMAZING!!! This pasta was so tasty and had so many different flavors. The olives and capers added just the right amount of zing and the feta pulled everything together. Best part, the spinach wasn't slimy or gross, it actually added a lot to the pasta, don't leave it out! Enjoy! (This one comes from the Cooking Club)

Ingredients

8 oz. rotini or fusilli (spiral pasta)
2 Tbsp. olive oil
1 medium onion, chopped
1 (14.5oz) can diced tomatoes with garlic, basil and oregano (I just had plain canned tomatoes and added the herbs separately)
½ C coarsely chopped pitted Kalamata olives
1 Tbsp. capers, rinsed
1 (6-oz.) pkg. baby spinach (I used a few handfuls fresh spinach - torn)
1 (4-oz.) pkg. crumbled feta cheese

Directions

Cook pasta according to package directions; drain

Meanwhile, heat oil in deep large skillet over medium heat until hot. Cook onion 4 to 5 minutes or until softened, stirring occasionally. Add tomatoes, olives and capers. Reduce heat to low; simmer 5 to 7 minutes or until slightly thickened.

Stir in spinach; cook, covered, 2 minutes or until wilted. Toss with pasta; sprinkle with cheese.

Makes 4-5 servings

Chez Diana

Fried Rice

3 c. cold cooked rice (it's important that the rice be well refrigerated, use
GOOD rice not instant, it can be made days ahead)

Ingredients

3 eggs
$1/8$ tsp. pepper
3 tbsp. peanut oil
2 tsp. grated fresh ginger
8 oz. pork, beef, or chicken, cut into VERY TINY cubes
8 green onion, finely chopped
1 carrot, finely chopped
1 stalk celery, finely chopped
½ yellow summer squash, finely chopped
5 or 6 fresh mushrooms, sliced
¼ c. frozen peas
½ zucchini, finely chopped

Directions

Heat wok VERY HOT. Add peanut oil and cook pork (beef or chicken)
quickly. Remove to bowl; cover with foil and set aside. Pour out any
liquid left in wok, allow to heat again to MEDIUM HOT and cook bacon
(do not let it get too crisp). Put cooked bacon in bowl with meat and
drain all fat, except 1 tablespoon. Beat eggs with pepper and pour $1/3$
egg mixture into wok, rotating wok to allow egg to form a very thin
"crepe".

Use wooden spatula to roll egg into a tube shape and remove from wok.
Chop into small pieces and add to bowl of meat. Repeat 2 more times to
use balance of egg mixture. Allow wok to get VERY HOT and add more
oil and fresh ginger. Put all vegetables in and cook only until slightly
tender. Add to bowl with meat. Allow wok to get VERY HOT again; add
a little more oil and put cold rice in wok. Cook, turning constantly, until
heated through. Add all cooked ingredients from bowl and season to
taste with soy sauce. Blend together in wok and serve immediately.
Meats and vegetables can be substituted to suit the family's taste. It is
very important that good rice be used (it should be "sticky" not loose
individual grains) and it is important to have all ingredients chopped and
ready before beginning to cook.

This recipe makes a generous main dish for a family of five.

Oven Brown Rice
Preheat oven to 375 degrees

1 cup brown rice
2 cups boiling water
2 tsp. vegetable oil
½ tsp. salt

Spray 8 inch square baking dish with cooking spray. Boil water. Pour water, oil and salt onto rice. Stir. Pour into baking dish, cover with aluminum foil. Bake for 1 hour. Fluff rice before serving.

Oriental Rice
(Pictured)
From "Controlling Your Fat Tooth" cookbook by Joseph C. Piscatella
This is great with stir fry!

1 tsp. olive oil or vegetable oil
1 small onion, chopped
2 cloves garlic, minced
1 cup long grain white rice
3 cups beef broth
1 tsp. paprika
1 tsp. soy sauce
2 Tbsp. chopped parsley

In a non-stick pan heat oil. Add onion and garlic and sauté until onion is crisp tender, 4-6 minutes. Add rice and brown 2-3, minutes. Add beef broth, paprika, and soy sauce and bring to a boil. Reduce heat, cover and simmer for 20-30 minutes or until broth is absorbed and rice is tender. Add parsley and toss before serving.

Makes 3 cups

Chez Diana

Gourmet Mushroom Risotto

Prep Time: 20 Min; Cook Time: 30 Min; Ready In: 50 Min
Original Recipe Yield 6 servings

Ingredients

6 cups chicken broth, divided
3 tablespoons olive oil, divided
1 pound portobello mushrooms, thinly sliced
1 pound white mushrooms, thinly sliced
2 shallots, diced
1 ½ cups Arborio rice
½ cup dry white wine
Sea salt to taste
freshly ground black pepper to taste
3 tablespoons finely chopped chives
4 tablespoons butter
1/3 cup freshly grated Parmesan cheese

Directions

In a saucepan, warm the broth over low heat. Warm 2 tablespoons olive oil in a large saucepan over medium-high heat.

Stir in the mushrooms, and cook until soft, about 3 minutes. Remove mushrooms and their liquid, and set aside. Add 1 tablespoon olive oil to skillet, and stir in the shallots. Cook 1 minute. Add rice, stirring to coat with oil, about 2 minutes.

When the rice has taken on a pale, golden color, pour in wine, stirring constantly until the wine is fully absorbed. Add ½ cup broth to the rice, and stir until the broth is absorbed. Continue adding broth ½ cup at a time, stirring continuously, until the liquid is absorbed and the rice is al dente, about 15 to 20 minutes. Remove from heat, and stir in mushrooms with their liquid, butter, chives, and parmesan. Season with salt and pepper to taste.

Mushroom Orzo Risotto

Linda Lau Anusasananan

Melt 1 tablespoon butter in a 12-inch frying pan over high heat. Add 12 ounces sliced mushrooms and ¾ cup chopped shallots or onion; cook, stirring often, until mushrooms are browned, 9 to 12 minutes. Reduce heat to medium & add 2 Tbsp butter and 2 cups orzo pasta; stir until pasta is golden, about 2 minutes. Add 3 cups chicken broth and ½ cup dry sherry. Bring to a boil over high heat, reduce heat and simmer, stirring often, until pasta is tender to bite and most of the liquid is absorbed, 9 to 11 minutes. If mixture becomes too thick before pasta is done, add a little more broth. Stir in 1/3 cup parmesan cheese and salt and pepper to taste. Spoon into bowls & sprinkle with a chopped parsley & more parmesan cheese to taste. Makes 3 or 4 main-dish servings.

Chez Diana

Three-Grain Rice

Orzo looks like short-grain rice, but is actually pasta.
This versatile ingredient can be substituted for rice in most recipes.
Southern Living 1995 Annual Recipes, page 166

Ingredients

$^2/_3$ cup orzo
2 Tbsp. vegetable oil
2 (14 ½-oz.) cans chicken broth
½ cup water
$^2/_3$ cup wild rice
$^2/_3$ cup long-grain rice
1 bay leaf
1 Tbsp. fresh thyme or 1 tsp. dried thyme
1 Tbsp. fresh sage or 1 tsp. dried sage
1 tsp. salt
¼ tsp. ground white pepper

Directions

Cook orzo in oil in a 3-quart saucepan over medium-high heat, stirring often, until lightly browned. Remove orzo from saucepan and set aside. Add chicken broth, water, and wild rice to saucepan; bring to a boil over medium heat. Cover, reduce heat, and simmer for 10 minutes. Stir in orzo, long-grain rice and remaining ingredients. Return to a boil; cover, reduce heat, and simmer 40 minutes or until moisture is absorbed and rice is tender. Remove from heat, and let stand 10 minutes. Remove and discard bay leaf.

Yield: 8 servings

Vegetables/Sides

Chez Diana

Artichoke and Kidney Bean Paella

A meatless twist on a traditional Spanish stovetop dish.
Prep Time: 10 min | Total Time: 35 min

1 tablespoon olive or vegetable oil
1 medium onion, chopped (½ cup)
2 garlic cloves, finely chopped
1 can (14 ounces) vegetable broth
1 cup uncooked regular long-grain
rice
1 cup frozen green peas
½ teaspoon ground turmeric
2 drops red pepper sauce
2 cups Progresso® red kidney
beans (from 19-oz can), drained,
rinsed
1 jar (6 ounces) marinated
artichoke hearts, drained

Heat oil in 12-inch skillet over medium-high heat. Cook onion and garlic in oil 3 to 4 minutes, stirring frequently, until crisp-tender. Stir in broth and rice. Heat to boiling; reduce heat. Cover and simmer 15 minutes.

Stir in remaining ingredients. Cook uncovered 5 to 10 minutes, stirring occasionally, until rice and peas are tender.

Makes: 4 servings

Roasted Asparagus with Feta
(Healthy recipe)

2 bunches medium asparagus, trimmed
2 tablespoons olive oil
½ teaspoon salt
¼ teaspoon freshly ground pepper
½ cup feta cheese, crumbled

Preheat oven to 500 degrees. Toss the asparagus with the olive oil, salt, and pepper in a shallow baking dish. Arrange it in a single layer. Roast for 8-10 minutes, shaking the pan halfway through, or until tender when pierced with a fork. Serve hot sprinkled with the feta.

Nutritional values per serving Calories: 103; Fat: 7 gm;
Saturated Fat: 2 gm; Cholesterol: 11 mg; Carbohydrate: 8 gm;
Fiber: 4 gm; Protein: 6 gm; Sodium: 337 mg

Chez Diana

Spicy Green Beans with Garlic

Recipe courtesy Emeril Lagasse, 2006
(Pictured)

¼ cup clarified butter or vegetable oil
3 cloves garlic, thinly sliced
2 small green peppers such as jalapeno or serrano, stems and seeds
  removed, minced
2 teaspoons turmeric powder
2 teaspoons ground cumin
$^1/_8$ teaspoon cayenne
1 pound green beans, tough ends removed
¼ cup water
1 ½ teaspoons salt
3 tablespoons sesame seeds

In a large saute pan, heat the butter or oil over medium-high heat. Add
the garlic, peppers, turmeric, cumin, and cayenne, and cook, stirring,
until the garlic begins to turn golden, about 2 minutes. Add the green
beans, water, salt, and stir well. Cover and cook over medium-low heat,
stirring occasionally, until the beans are tender, 4 to 5 minutes. Add
the sesame seeds and cook uncovered, stirring, until toasted, 2 to 3
minutes.

Remove from the heat and adjust seasoning, to taste.

Serves 4-6

Chez Diana

Green Bean Casserole

From "Favorite Brand Name Cookbook" by Consumers Guide

Ingredients
1 can cream of mushroom soup
½ c. milk
1 tsp. soy sauce
Dash pepper
2-9-oz. pkgs. Frozen French cut
  green beans
1 can (3 ½ oz.) French fried onions

Directions
Cook and drain green beans. In greased 1 ½ quart casserole, combine mushroom soup, milk, soy sauce, and pepper until smooth, then stir in green beans. Stir in ½ can of French fried onions. Bake at 350 degrees for 25 minutes. Top with the remaining French fried onions. Bake for 5 more minutes. Serve.

Broccoli and Peppers

Presented by: Better Homes and Gardens®
If you don't have a steamer basket, improvise with a metal
colander to prepare this healthful vegetable dish.

Ingredients
1 pound broccoli, cut into
  flowerets
1 medium red or yellow sweet
  pepper, cut into 1-inch pieces
2 tablespoons reduced-calorie
  margarine or regular margarine
1 tablespoon lemon juice
$\frac{1}{8}$ teaspoon pepper
1 teaspoon finely shredded lemon
  peel

Directions
1. Place broccoli and pepper in a steamer basket over simmering water. Steam, covered, for 8 to 12 minutes or until vegetables are crisp-tender. Drain.
2. Arrange on a serving platter. Meanwhile, in a small saucepan melt the margarine. Stir in lemon peel, lemon juice, and pepper.

Drizzle over broccoli mixture.

6 Servings

Chez Diana

Curried Cabbage

From Readers Digest "Great Recipes for Good Health" Cookbook
Preparation: 10 minutes | Cooking Time: 23 minutes

1 small head green cabbage
 (about 1 pound)
1 Tbsp. unsalted margarine
2 tsp. mustard seeds
2 medium sized yellow onions,
 sliced thin
2 tsp. curry powder
¼ cup water

Cut the cabbage into wedges, cut out and discard the white core, and slice each wedge ⅛ inch thick. Set aside. In heavy skillet, melt

margarine over moderate heat; add the mustard seeds and cook covered until they begin to sputter. Add the onions and cook, uncovered until soft, about 5 minutes.
Stir in the curry powder and cook 1 minute. Add the cabbage and water, cover, cook for 15 minutes or until cabbage is tender.

Serves 4

Corn Pudding

From Readers Digest "Great Recipes for Good Health" Cookbook
Preparation: 10 minutes | Cooking Time: 1 hour
Preheat oven to 350 degrees

1 large egg
1 large egg white
1 cup skim milk
2 Tbsp. flour
¼ tsp. baking powder
⅛ tsp. pepper
1 ½ cup fresh or frozen corn
2 green onions, chopped fine
2 tsp. Parmesan cheese
Nonstick cooking spray

In a medium size bowl, whisk together the egg, egg white, milk,

flour, baking powder, and pepper. Stir in the corn, green onions and cheese. Coat a nine inch pie pan with cooking spray. Add the corn mixture and set the pie pan in a shallow baking pan. Add enough hot water to the baking pan to come halfway up the sides of the pie pan. Bake, uncovered for 1 to 1 ¼ hours or until a knife inserted in the center comes out clean and the pudding is puffed and golden.
Serves 4

Chez Diana

Candied Carrots

From "Cooking In Style" Cookbook By Charlotte Adams

Ingredients
6 medium carrots, peeled and cut
Boiling salted water
¼ cup butter
¼ cup brown sugar

Directions
Cook carrots in boiling salted water until tender (6 to 8 minutes). Drain well. Melt butter, add carrots, and sprinkle with the brown sugar. Heat, stirring frequently, until sugar is melted and carrots are well coated with the mixture.

Serves 4

Parsley Braised Celery

From "Cooking In Style" Cookbook By Charlotte Adams

1 medium bunch Pascal celery
Beef or chicken stock
1 Tbsp. fresh chopped parsley
2 Tbsp. butter
¼ tsp. salt
Dash freshly ground pepper

Wash celery and cut ribs into 2 inch lengths.

Cook in beef or chicken stock to depth of 1 inch in a covered saucepan, 18-20 minutes or until celery is tender. Drain if necessary. Add parsley, butter, salt and pepper. Toss lightly. Serve hot.

Serves 6

Baked Crushed Corn

Preheat oven to 350 degrees

Ingredients
1 can crushed corn
3 eggs
1 cup milk
3 Tbsp. flour
Sugar to taste
Salt to taste
4 Tbsp. melted butter

Directions
Combine all ingredients except butter. Pour into a greased casserole dish. Pour melted butter on top.

Bake at 350 degrees for 45 minutes to an hour. Serve immediately.

Chez Diana

Classic Baked Corn Pudding

Creamy corn bakes into old-fashioned comfort food.
This cheesy version is a mainstay for many family gatherings.
Prep Time: 20 min | Total Time: 1 hour 35 min | Makes: 16 servings (½ cup each)

Ingredients

½ cup butter or margarine
1 small onion, chopped (¼ cup)
½ cup all-purpose flour
½ teaspoon salt
½ teaspoon pepper
4 cups milk (1 quart)
6 eggs, slightly beaten
2 cups shredded Cheddar cheese (8 oz)
2 bags (12 oz) frozen corn, thawed, drained
½ cup chopped fresh parsley or 2 tablespoon parsley flakes
¾ cup plain bread crumbs
3 tablespoons butter or margarine, melted

Directions

Preheat oven to 350°F. Spray 13x9-inch (3-quart) glass baking dish or
3-quart casserole with cooking spray. In 4-quart Dutch oven, melt ½
cup butter over medium heat. Add onion; cook 3 to 4 minutes, stirring
frequently, until tender. Stir in flour, salt and pepper until well blended.
Stir in milk. Cook 4 to 5 minutes, stirring constantly, until thickened.
Gradually stir in eggs and cheese. Stir in corn and parsley. Pour into
baking dish. In small bowl, mix bread crumbs and 3 tablespoons melted
butter; sprinkle over corn mixture.

Bake uncovered 55 to 65 minutes or until mixture is set and knife
Inserted in center comes out clean. Let stand 5 to 10 minutes before
serving.

Substitution-You can use three 15.25-ounce cans of whole kernel corn,
drained, instead of frozen corn.

Chez Diana

A Corn Side Dish

Created by The MDM Team, Tuesday, November 13, 2007
A great and easy vegetable side to go with your meal.

Ingredients

1 (10 oz.) package frozen corn
1 (8 oz.) can tomato sauce
1 (4 oz.) can mushroom stems and pieces, drained
1 tomato, finely chopped (med to large)
$^1/_3$ cup celery, finely chopped
$^1/_3$ cup green peppers, finely chopped
2 tsp. olive oil
2 tbsp. brown sugar
1 tsp. onion powder
1 tsp. garlic powder
½ tsp. salt
1 dash black pepper
1 dash cayenne pepper (optional)

Directions

1. In 2-½ to 3 qt casserole dish, toss celery and green pepper in oil.
2. Microwave on high for 2 minutes.
3. Mix in all rest of ingredients.
4. Cover and cook on medium high until done for 9-10 minutes.

Additional Tips

As microwaves can vary in strength, you may want to check it the first time you do it.

Spicy, Smoky Cauliflower Mash

Food Network.Com Recipe Courtesy of Ingrid Hoffmann

Ingredients

4 cups cauliflower florets (about 1 large head)
1 cup grated mozzarella cheese
½ cup milk
3 Tbsp. sour cream
1 Tbsp. lime juice (½ lime)
1-2 tsp. adobo sauce, to taste
Salt
Freshly ground pepper
Cilantro, chopped, for garnish

Directions

Steam the cauliflower in a steamer insert over boiling water, covered, until it is very soft, 15-20 minutes. Transfer the steamed cauliflower to a blender and puree with the cheese, milk, sour cream and lime juice until smooth. Add the adobo sauce, salt and pepper to taste. Pulse a few more times to mix. Transfer to a serving bowl. Sprinkle with the cilantro and serve.

Serves 4

Curried Cauliflower

Ingredients

2 Tbsp. vegetable oil
½ head cauliflower (about 3 cups)
 separated into 1 ½ inch florets
1 tsp. cumin
1 tsp. coriander
¼ tsp. turmeric
$^1/_3$ tsp. cayenne pepper
½ tsp. fennel seeds, toasted and
 ground
Water
1 Tbsp. lemon juice
Salt, to taste

Serve 4

Directions

Heat the oil in a large sauté pan over high heat. Add the cauliflower and sauté for several minutes. Season with salt. Add the cumin, coriander, turmeric, cayenne pepper and fennel seeds (or you can use 1 ½ tsp. curry powder). Saute 1 minute more and add 3 Tbsp. water. Cover and cook for 6-7 minutes more over medium high heat, stirring occasionally. Cook until cauliflower has softened and there is no more liquid. Add more water in 1 tablespoon increments if needed to avoid scorching. Add lemon juice and serve.

Blanquette of Mushrooms in Casserole

From "Cooking In Style" Cookbook By Charlotte Adams

Ingredients

1 ½ lbs. medium mushrooms
1 ½ cups dry white wine
 (approximately)
1 bay leaf
Salt and Pepper to taste
2 Tbsp. butter
2 Tbsp. flour
Minced parsley

Serves 4

Directions

Wash mushrooms. Place in a 3 quart casserole and pour on enough wine to not quite cover them. Add bay leaf, salt and pepper. Cook until the mushrooms are done (about 10 minutes). Remove mushrooms and reduce liquid over high heat to half original quantity. Melt butter and stir in flour smoothly. Add reduced liquid to butter mixture and stir until thickened. Add mushrooms, sprinkle with parsley, and serve.

Chez Diana

Broiled Ranch Mushrooms

From "Favorite Brand Name Recipes"

Ingredients

1 lb. medium mushrooms
1 pck. (1 oz.) Hidden Valley Ranch Salad Dressing and Seasoning Mix
¼ cup vegetable oil
¼ cup water
1 Tbsp. balsamic vinegar

Makes 4 Servings

Directions

Place mushrooms in a gallon size plastic bag. Whisk together salad dressing mix, oil, water and vinegar. Pour over mushrooms. Seal bag and marinate in the refrigerator for 30 minutes, turning occasionally. Place mushrooms on a broiling rack. Broil 4 inches from heat for about 8 minutes or until tender. Serve hot.

Vidalia Onion Casserole

Printed from COOKS.COM

Ingredients

½ c. butter
4 med. Vidalia onions, sliced into ¼ inch rings
15 Saltine crackers, crushed
1 can cream of mushroom soup
2 eggs, beaten
½ to $^1/_3$ c. milk
1 c. shredded sharp Cheddar cheese

Directions

Melt butter in large fry pan, saute onions over medium heat until clear. Reserve 3 tablespoons of cracker crumbs for topping and place remaining crumbs in the bottom of a lightly greased 2 quart casserole. Remove onions from pan with a slotted spoon. Add soup and onions in alternating layers until full. Combine eggs and milk, pour on onions. Top with cheese and remaining cracker crumbs. Bake at 350 degrees for 20 to 30 minutes or until brown and bubbly. Serves 4 to 6.

Chez Diana

Baked Tomatoes
From "Cooking In Style" Cookbook By Charlotte Adams

Ingredients
6 ripe medium tomatoes
Seasoned salt
Freshly ground black pepper
¼ cup minced onion
2 Tbsp. sugar
2 Tbsp. dried basil (or ¼ cup fresh basil)
Prepared poultry stuffing
Butter

Directions
Wash tomatoes, remove stems, cut in half through the center. Arrange in a shallow baking dish, cut side up. Put enough water to just cover the bottom of the dish. Sprinkle each tomato half with seasoned salt and pepper. Place a teaspoon of onion on each. Sprinkle with sugar and basil and cover with stuffing. Dot with butter. Bake in 375 degree oven until nicely browned (30 minutes).

Serves 6

Minted Peas
From 1987 Southern Living Cookbook
Cathy Powell, Claxton, Georgia

Ingredients
2 ½ pounds English peas
2 Tbsp. jellied mint sauce
1 Tbsp. butter or margarine
½ tsp. salt
¼ tsp. pepper

Directions
Cook peas in boiling water to cover for 10 to 12 minutes, or until tender. Drain, reserving ¼ cup liquid. Return peas and reserved liquid to pan and add remaining ingredients. Cook over medium heat, stirring constantly, 2-3 minutes, or until mint sauce melts.

Yield: 4 servings

Chez Diana

Veggie Casserole
By Kathie

Layered veggies and cheese and soup-sour cream mixture make
this a quick and easy dish for a holiday meal or gathering

Ingredients

1 can french style cut green beans
(regular can be used) drained
1 can corn drained
1 can sliced water chestnuts
drained
1 can cream of celery soup
(chicken or mushroom work also)
1 cup sour cream
1 cup shredded cheese (cheddar,
or american or your favorite
cheese)
1 sleeve of Ritz style crackers
crushed
1 stick of margarine, melted
½ cup chopped onion

Directions

Layer green beans and corn in a
13x9 casserole. Mix sour cream
and soup, layer half on top. Sprinkle
water chestnuts and onion over all.
Layer rest of soup mixture. Sprinkle
cheese, then crushed crackers.
Pour melted butter over all. Bake
at 350 degrees for about 40
minutes or until bubbly and
slightly golden brown.

Prep Time: 15 Min
Cook Time: 40 Min

Servings: 8

Batter Fried Zucchini

From Nancy Gaifyllia, former About.com Guide
The key to great crispy zucchini is to slice it thinly and fry at high heat
so the zucchini has time to fry but not to absorb a lot of oil. Use a cheese
slicer, mandolin, or long bladed knife to get uniformly thin slices.

Ingredients

1 large zucchini, washed, trimmed
and cut lengthwise into ¹/₈ to ³/₁₆
inch thick rounds
olive oil for frying
½ tsp. salt

For batter:
8 oz. club soda
½ tsp. sea salt
¾ cup + 1 Tbsp. all purpose flour

Directions

Salt zucchini and let sit for 20
minutes. Make batter by pouring
soda water into a bowl and stirring
in the flour and salt slowly using a
whisk to mix. Bring oil to high heat.
Coat the zucchini in the batter,
place in the oil to fry 5-6 minutes,
until golden on both sides and
batter puffs up. Drain on absorbent
toweling just long enough to remove
excess oil. Serve hot. Serves 4 as a
side dish, 6 as an appetizer.

Potatoes

Chez Diana

Oven Roasted Potatoes

By: JMRYGH
"A great roasted potato side dish made with olive oil and herbs."
Pictured on Potatoes chapter page.
Prep Time: 15 | MinCook Time: 30

Ingredients

¹/₈ cup olive oil
1 tablespoon minced garlic
½ teaspoon dried basil
½ teaspoon dried marjoram
½ teaspoon dried dill weed
½ teaspoon dried thyme
½ teaspoon dried oregano
½ teaspoon dried parsley
½ teaspoon crushed red pepper
  flakes
½ teaspoon salt
4 large potatoes, peeled
  and cubed

Directions

1. Preheat oven to 475 degrees F
2. In a large bowl, combine oil, garlic, basil, marjoram, dill weed, thyme, oregano, parsley, red pepper flakes, and salt. Stir in potatoes until evenly coated. Place potatoes in a single layer on a roasting pan or baking sheet.
3. Roast for 20 to 30 minutes in the preheated oven, turning occasionally to brown on all sides.

Yield 4 servings

Onion Soup Mix Oven Roasted Potatoes

Ingredients

1 env. Lipton onion soup mix
2 lbs. potatoes, cut in lg. chunks
¹/₃ c. olive oil or vegetable oil

Directions

Preheat oven to 450 degrees. In a plastic bag, add all ingredients. Close bag and shake until potatoes are evenly coated. Empty potatoes into shallow baking or roasting pan; discard bag. Bake, stirring occasionally, 40 minutes or until potatoes are tender and golden brown. Garnish, if desired, with chopped parsley.

8 servings

Chez Diana

Make Ahead Mashed Potatoes

© Stephanie Gallagher Nov 21, 2006
Potatoes with cream cheese, sour cream and garlic you can make
a day ahead. It's the perfect Thanksgiving or Christmas side dish recipe.

12 cups Yukon gold potatoes
(approximately 9 potatoes),
peeled and cubed
6 cloves garlic
6 oz low fat cream cheese
1 cup nonfat sour cream
2 Tbsp. butter
salt and pepper to taste

Serves 12

Put potatoes and garlic in a large pot. Cover with water. Add a dash of salt. Bring to a boil and cook until potatoes are fork-tender, about 15 minutes. Drain potatoes, and transfer to a large bowl. Add cream cheese, sour cream, butter and salt and pepper, mashing lightly, until smooth. Be careful not to overmash. Transfer to a 9 X 13 baking dish that has been sprayed with nonstick cooking spray. Cover and refrigerate overnight. Preheat oven to 350 degrees. Bake potatoes for 30 minutes.

Per serving: 178 calories, 5 g fat, 15 mg cholesterol, 256 mg sodium, 30 g carbohydrate,
2 g fiber, 5 g protein, 6% Vitamin A, 26% Vitamin C, 5% calcium, 4% iron

Delicious Oven French Fries (Healthy recipe)

4 large potatoes (2 pounds)
1 teaspoon hot pepper flakes
1 teaspoon garlic powder
1 teaspoon onion powder
¼ teaspoon salt
1 teaspoon white pepper
¼ teaspoon allspice
8 cups ice water
1 tablespoon vegetable oil

Makes 5 servings.

Scrub potatoes and cut into long
½-inch strips. Place potato strips
into ice water, cover, and chill for

1 hour or longer. Remove potatoes and dry strips thoroughly. Place garlic powder, onion powder, salt, white pepper, allspice, and pepper flakes in a plastic bag. Toss potatoes in spice mixture. Brush potatoes with oil, and place in a nonstick shallow baking pan. Cover with aluminum foil and place in a 475-degree oven for 15 minutes. Remove foil and continue baking for an additional 15 to 20 minutes or until golden brown. Turn fries occasionally to brown on all sides.

Chez Diana

Whipped Yukon Gold Potatoes with Horseradish

The slightly tangy horseradish flavor of these potatoes pairs well with gravy.

Recipe Ingredients

5 pounds Yukon Gold potatoes
3 tablespoons salt
½ pound (16 tablespoons) unsalted butter
1 ½ cups light cream
White pepper to taste
6 ounces prepared horseradish

Directions

Peel and quarter the potatoes and cover with cold water. You can hold the potatoes this way at room temperature for 6 hours ahead of cooking (or for a day ahead in the refrigerator).

Drain the potatoes, put them in a 6-qt. pot, and cover with water. Add 1 tablespoon salt. Bring to boil, reduce to a gentle boil, and cook until fork-tender, 25 to 30 minutes. Pour off the water and let the potatoes cool. (If they sit in water off the heat, they'll turn pasty.)

In an electric mixer with the whisk attachment, whip the potatoes until smooth, about 1 minute; add the butter and mix until melted and combined, about 30 seconds. Add the cream, 2 tablespoons salt, and pepper to taste; whip until smooth and creamy, about 2 min., scraping down the sides of the bowl frequently. (You can also use a food mill.) Fold in the horseradish and combine well.

To Keep The Potatoes Warm: Put an inch of water in the pot the potatoes were cooked in and set over low heat. Put the potatoes in a stainless-steel mixing bowl, cover with foil, and put the bowl on top of the pot. You can hold the potatoes like this for at least 2 hours; just maintain the water level and keep the heat low.

Big Martha's Mashed Potatoes with Cream Cheese

This delicious recipe for mashed potatoes came from
Martha's mother, Mrs. Kostyra. Serves 8

3 ½ pounds white or Yukon Gold
  potatoes
Coarse salt and freshly ground pepper
8 ounces cream cheese, softened
4 ounces (1 stick) unsalted butter,
  softened
¼ cup whole milk, warmed
½ cup heavy cream, warmed

Place potatoes and 1 tablespoon salt
in a medium pot, cover with cold
water by 2 inches, and bring to a
boil. Reduce heat, cover partially, and
simmer until potatoes are tender,
about 35 minutes.

Drain, and let stand until just cool
enough to handle. Rub off skins,
and discard. Cut potatoes into large
pieces. Combine potatoes, cream
cheese, butter, milk, and ¼ cup cream
in a mixer bowl fitted with the paddle
attachment. Beat until combined.
Season with salt and pepper, and beat
to desired consistency. Return mashed
potatoes to pot, and place over
medium heat. Add remaining cream,
and cook, stirring constantly, until
heated through. Serve immediately,
or keep warm in a covered bowl over
simmering water for up to 2 hours.

Quick Twice Baked Potatoes

Idaho baking potatoes, 1 per person
2 tbsp. Bacos (or substitute ½ cup
  chopped crab meat)
½ cup Shredded Cheddar cheese
2 tbsp. chopped chives
½ cup sour cream
Salt and pepper to taste

Wash potatoes thoroughly. Then
poke a few holes in each one with
a fork. On a microwave plate, place
one paper towel, and place potatoes
in circle at the outside edge of the
plate, pointing toward center. Nuke
10 minutes on high, turning every 3
minutes if microwave does not rotate.

While microwave is running, preheat oven to 450 degrees. Remove
potatoes from microwave and cool
quickly under running water. Cut in
half and scoop out potato, leaving ¼
inch of potato in the shell.
Place scooped potato in mixing
bowl (if using crab, discard ¼ of the
scooped potato). Add sour cream and
mash scooped potato until smooth.
Gently stir in bacos, shredded cheese,
chopped chives, finely chopped crab
meat or whatever you like and re-stuff
potatoes. Place potatoes on baking
sheet and bake in oven for 15 minutes
or until top begins to brown.

Chez Diana

Sweet Potato Hash

Recipe courtesy of Chef Robert Childers,
House of Blues, Chicago, Illinois

Ingredients

1 ½ pounds sweet potatoes, peeled
and ½-inch diced
2 tablespoons salted butter
2 tablespoons vegetable oil
1 cup ½-inch diced onion
1 cup ½-inch diced celery
2 cloves garlic, minced
1 cup ½-inch diced red bell pepper
1 cup ½-inch diced green bell pepper
¼ teaspoon crushed red pepper flakes
salt and freshly ground black pepper

Directions

Place the diced potatoes in a
medium pot, cover with 2 inches of
cold water, and generously season
with salt. Over high heat bring to
a boil, reduce the heat to medium,
and simmer for 5 minutes. Drain
and set aside. In a large non-stick
skillet over medium heat, melt the
butter and heat the oil. Add the
onion and celery and cook for 10
minutes, until the onions are soft.
Add the garlic and continue to cook
for 3 minutes, stirring constantly.
Add the red and green peppers,
and red pepper flakes, and continue
to cook for 5 minutes. Add the
potatoes and cook until they are just
heated through, about 1 minute.
Season with salt and pepper to taste.
Serve hot.

Yield: Serves 6

Diana's Favorite Mashed Sweet Potatoes

Ingredients

2 or 3 large sweet potatoes –
peeled and cut into 1 in chunks
3 T. butter
Juice from ½ lemon
¼ c brown sugar
2 T. Karo Syrup
1 tsp. vanilla
¼ tsp. nutmeg

Directions

Place sweet potatoes in cold salted
water and bring to boil. Cook 15
minutes. Remove & drain.

Put remaining ingredients in small
microwave bowl and microwave
and stir.

With electric mixer beat potatoes
and syrup mixture until thoroughly
mashed.

Serve immediately.

Chez Diana

Sweet Potato Oven Fries

1/2004

Take care to cut the potatoes into evenly sized wedges so that all of the pieces will cook at about the same rate. Although it isn't required, a nonstick baking sheet works particularly well for this recipe. It not only keeps the fries from sticking to the pan but, because of its dark color, encourages deep and even browning. Whether you choose a nonstick baking sheet or a regular baking sheet, make sure that it is heavy duty. The intense heat of the oven may cause lighter pans to warp. When buying sweet potatoes for oven fries, try to choose those with a uniform shape. When peeling, shave away odd bumps and curves to make them even more uniform. Because sweet potatoes have more sugar and moisture than russets, the fries will not be as crisp, but they are tasty nonetheless.

Ingredients

2 sweet potatoes (about 13 to 15 ounces each), peeled, each potato
   cut lengthwise into evenly sized wedges
5 tablespoons vegetable oil or peanut oil
Table salt and ground black pepper

Directions

1. Adjust oven rack to lowest position; heat oven to 475 degrees. Place potatoes in large bowl and toss with one tablespoon oil; soak 10 minutes. Meanwhile, coat 18 by 12-inch heavy-duty rimmed baking sheet (see note) with 4 remaining tablespoons oil and sprinkle evenly with ¾ teaspoon salt and ¼ teaspoon pepper; set aside.

2. Arrange potatoes in single layer on prepared baking sheet; bake until bottoms of potatoes are spotty golden brown, about 25 minutes, rotating baking sheet after 10 minutes. Using metal spatula and tongs, scrape to loosen potatoes from pan, then flip each wedge, keeping potatoes in single layer. Continue baking until fries are completely golden brown, 5 to 15 minutes longer, rotating pan as needed if fries are browning unevenly.

3. Transfer fries to second baking sheet lined with paper towels to drain. Season with additional salt and pepper to taste and serve.

Serves 3 to 4

Sweet Potato And Sausage Hash

Rachael Ray Preparation Time: 10 minutes; Cook Time: 25 minutes

Ingredients

2 large sweet potatoes (2 lbs.)
  peeled and cut into ½ inch pieces
½ lb. bulk sausage
2 Tbsp. vegetable oil
2 bell peppers, any color
1 onion, chopped
2 cloves garlic, minced
2 tsp. ground cumin
Salt and pepper
Salsa, for Serving

In medium pot of boiling salted water cook the sweet potatoes until almost tender, about 4 minutes. Drain and set aside. In a large skillet, cook the sausage over medium heat until browned and crumbly, about 10 minutes. Transfer to colander to drain. Heat the oil over medium high heat. Add the onions, garlic, and bell peppers and cook until softened, about 5 minutes. Add the sausage, the cumin and sweet potatoes and cook for 5 minutes more. Season to taste with salt and pepper.

Serve with salsa.

Yummy Sweet Potato Casserole

By: TINA B "My family begs me to make this creamy baked dish every Thanksgiving and Christmas. What makes it so good is the pecan topping! Try it and I'm sure it will become your new tradition!" Prep Time: 30 Min; Cook Time: 30 Min; Ready In: 1 Hr | Servings 12 Original Recipe Yield 6 cups

Ingredients

4 cups sweet potato, cubed
½ cup white sugar
2 eggs, beaten
½ teaspoon salt
4 tablespoons butter, softened
½ cup milk
½ teaspoon vanilla extract
½ cup packed brown sugar
$^1/_3$ cup all-purpose flour
3 tablespoons butter, softened
½ cup chopped pecans

Directions

Preheat oven to 325 degrees F (165 degrees C). Put sweet potatoes in a medium saucepan with water to cover. Cook over medium high heat until tender; drain and mash. In a large bowl, mix together the sweet potatoes, white sugar, eggs, salt, butter, milk and vanilla extract. Mix until smooth. Transfer to a 9x13 inch baking dish. In medium bowl, mix the brown sugar and flour. Cut in the butter until the mixture is coarse. Stir in the pecans. Sprinkle the mixture over the sweet potato mixture. Bake in preheated oven 30 minutes, or until the topping is lightly brown

Chez Diana

Smashed Potatoes

White potatoes can be used instead of Red Bliss, but their skins lack the rosy color of Red Bliss skins. Try to get potatoes of equal size; if that's not possible, test the larger potatoes for doneness. If only larger potatoes are available, increase the cooking time by about 10 minutes. Check for doneness with a paring knife.

Ingredients

2 pounds Red Bliss potatoes (about 2 inches in diameter), unpeeled and scrubbed
Table salt
1 bay leaf
4 tablespoons unsalted butter melted and warm
½ cup cream cheese (4 ounces), at room temperature
Ground black pepper
3 tablespoons chopped fresh chives (optional)

Place potatoes in large saucepan and cover with 1 inch cold water; add 1 teaspoon salt and bay leaf. Bring to boil over high heat, then reduce heat to medium-low and simmer gently until paring knife can be inserted into potatoes with no resistance, 35 to 45 minutes. Reserve ½ cup cooking water, then drain potatoes. Return potatoes to pot, discard bay leaf and allow potatoes to stand in pot, uncovered, until surfaces are dry, about 5 minutes.

While potatoes dry, whisk melted butter and softened cream cheese in medium bowl until smooth and fully incorporated. Add ¼ cup of reserved cooking water, ½ teaspoon pepper, chives (if using), and ½ teaspoon salt. Using rubber spatula or back of wooden spoon, smash potatoes just enough to break skins. Fold in butter/cream cheese mixture until most of liquid has been absorbed and chunks of potatoes remain. Add more cooking water 1 tablespoon at a time as needed; until potatoes are slightly looser than desired (potatoes will thicken slightly with standing). Adjust seasonings with salt and pepper; serve immediately.

STEP BY STEP: Making Smashed Potatoes

1. For the best flavor and texture, boil whole, skin on potatoes. Leave a measuring cup nearby as a reminder to reserve some cooking liquid.
2. While the potatoes are drying, whisk together the cream cheese and butter.
3. When smashing the potatoes, use a spatula or large wooden spoon; both work better than a potato masher or a fork. Smash just until the skins are broken.
4. Fold the cream cheese mixture into the potatoes gently; adding more reserved cooking liquid if the potatoes look dry.

Serves 4 to 6

Chez Diana

Twice Baked Rosemary Blue Potato Mash

Recipe courtesy Claire Robinson, 2010

Yield: 4 servings | Times: Prep 15 min | Inactive Prep

Cook 30 min | Total: 45 min

Ingredients

6 tablespoons unsalted butter, plus more for baking dish
2 cloves garlic, peeled and smashed
1 tablespoon finely chopped rosemary leaves
Freshly cracked black pepper
6 Yukon gold potatoes, peeled and cut into chunks
Kosher salt
1 ¼ cups crumbled blue cheese

Directions

Butter or spray a 6 to 8 cup shallow baking dish.

In a small saucepan, heat the butter, garlic, rosemary and pepper, to taste, until the butter is melted. Allow it to sit over very low heat to infuse flavors and keep hot while cooking the potatoes.

In a large pot, add the potatoes, cover with water and add a heavy pinch of salt. Bring to a boil over medium heat, then reduce the heat and simmer the potatoes until fork tender, about 15 minutes. Immediately drain the potatoes and then put them back into hot pot over very low heat, to dry thoroughly. Next, mash or use a ricer

Remove the smashed garlic from warm butter and whisk in about 1 cup of the blue cheese. By hand, mix the cheese sauce into the potatoes and season with a little salt and pepper, to taste. Spread into the prepared baking dish and top with remaining cheese. Broil until the cheese is golden and melting, about 3 minutes. Remove the potatoes from the oven and serve.

Desserts

Chez Diana

Chocolate & Peanut Butter Chip Cookies

Ingredients

2 sticks butter, softened (no substitutes)
2 whole eggs
4 cups Bisquick
2 cups halved walnuts [chopped?]
2 cups halved pecans [chopped?]
2 cups peanut butter chips
2 cups semi-sweet chips

Directions

Beat together first three ingredients. Add chunky stuff and mix.
Scoop one teaspoon of batter and shape into a ball.
Drop onto an ungreased cookie sheet. Repeat.
Bake at 375° for 8 minutes. **Will burn easily!**
Makes about 5 dozen.

Rita Sala Cookies

From John's Cousin Rita

Ingredients

3 eggs
1 ¼ lbs. flour
1 tsp. baking soda
1 tsp. baking powder
¾ lb. of sugar
½ lb. butter
3 Tbsp. pine nuts
½ bag yeast
6 Tbsp. raisins, soaked in warm water & 2 Tbsp. marsala- drained, dried
  & dusted with flour
Corn flakes

Directions

Mix dough. Drop by teaspoonful into corn flakes and roll. Place 3 inches apart on baking sheet. Bake at 350 degrees for 15 minutes. Let cool.

Chez Diana

Potato Chip Cookies

(Pictured)

The Washington Post, December 13, 2006

This is a buttery, shortbread-like cookie. Potato chips add to the texture
and provide salt. Store the cookies in an airtight container for up to 3 days.
They can be frozen, well wrapped, for up to 1 month.

Ingredients

2 sticks (8 ounces) unsalted butter, at room temperature
½ cup sugar
1 ¾ cups flour
¾ cup coarsely crushed potato chips
1 teaspoon vanilla extract
1 cup confectioners' sugar, for dusting

Directions

Preheat the oven to 350 degrees. Line several large baking sheets with
parchment paper.

In a large bowl, using a stand mixer or electric hand mixer, beat the
butter and sugar on medium-high speed for several minutes, until light
and fluffy. Stop to scrape down the sides of the bowl. Reduce the speed
to low and add the flour, crushed potato chips and vanilla extract,

mixing well. Drop
rounded tablespoons,
spaced about 2 inches
apart, onto the baking
sheets. The cookies will
spread slightly. Bake for
8 to 10 minutes or until
the edges are barely
browned. Cool on the
baking sheets for 5
minutes, then transfer the
cookies to wire racks to
cool completely. Sprinkle
confectioners' sugar

through a sieve or place it in a shallow bowl and coat the cooled cookies
evenly to the desired level of sweetness. Recipe Source: Adapted from
"Columbus Cookbook" (Visitors Center, Columbus, Ind., 1987).

Makes 42 to 48 cookies

Chez Diana

Chocolate Chip Pretzel Cookies

From Joanne Fluke's "The Plum Pudding Murder", *pp 126-128*
Preheat oven to 350 degrees F., Rack in the middle position.

1 cup softened butter (2 sticks, ½ pound)
2 cups white (granulated) sugar
3 Tablespoons molasses
2 teaspoons vanilla
1 teaspoon baking soda
2 beaten eggs (just whip them up in a glass with a fork)
2 cups crushed salted thin stick pretzels (measure AFTER crushing)
 (I used Snyder's)
2 and ½ cups all-purpose flour (pack it down in the cup when you measure it)
1 and ½ cups semi-sweet (the regular kind) chocolate chips
Note: If you can't find thin stick pretzels in your store, you can use the mini regular pretzels. Just make sure that any pretzels you use are SALTED.
Note: This dough gets really stiff—you might be better off using an electric mixer if you have one.

Mix the softened butter with the sugar and the molasses. Beat until the mixture is light and fluffy, and the molasses is completely mixed in. Add the vanilla and baking soda. Mix them in well. Break the eggs into a glass and whip them up with a fork. Add them to your bowl and mix until they're thoroughly incorporated. Put your pretzels in a zip lock plastic bag. Seal it carefully (you don't want crumbs all over your counter) and place it on a flat surface. Get out your rolling pin and run it over the bag, crushing the pretzels inside. Do this until there are no large pieces and the largest is a quarter-inch long. Measure out two cups of crushed pretzels and mix them into the dough in your bowl. Add one cup of flour and mix it in. Then add the second cup and mix thoroughly. Add the final half cup of flour and mix that in. Measure out a cup and a half of chocolate chips and add them to your cookie dough. If you're using an electric mixer, mix them in at the slowest speed. You can also put the mixer away, and stir in the chips by hand. Drop by rounded teaspoons onto greased (or sprayed with Pam or another nonstick cooking spray) cookie sheets. You can also line your cookie sheets with parchment paper, if you prefer. Place 12 cookies on each standard sized sheet. **Note:** I used a 2-teaspoon cookie disher to scoop out this dough. It's faster than doing it with a spoon. Bake the cookies at 350 degrees F. for 10 to 12 minutes or until nicely browned. (Mine took 11 minutes.) Let the cookies cool for two minutes and then remove them from the baking sheets. Transfer them to a wire rack to finish cooling. **Yield:** Approximately 5 dozen chewy, fairly soft chocolaty cookies.

Chez Diana

Pecan Butter Balls

From Ann Perlman's "The Christmas Cookie Club"

2 cups pecans, chopped
2 cups flour
1 cup melted butter
½ cup sugar
2 tsp. vanilla
¼ tsp. salt
Confectioner's sugar

Preheat oven to 325 degrees

Yield: 5 dozen

Combine all ingredients except confectioner's sugar. Gather dough into a ball. With floured hands shape into 1 inch balls & bake on ungreased cookie sheets lined with wax paper & sprayed with Pam. Bake 20-22 minutes. Pull papers and cookie from sheet unto cookie racks to cool slightly. While still warm shake them in a bag filled with Confectioner's sugar. Place them back on paper and add more Confectioners' sugar as they cool.

Buttery Pecan Rounds

From Ann Perlman's "The Christmas Cookie Club"
Double-Dipped Chocolate Peanut Butter Cookies

Pecan halves for tops
1 cup flour
½ tsp. salt
1 cup softened butter
¾ cup dark brown sugar
1 large egg yolk
²/₃ cup finely chopped pecans

Toast pecan halves at 350 degrees for 10 minutes. Cool. Preheat oven to 325 degrees.
Using electric mixer, cream the butter and sugar for 3 minutes.
Mix in the egg yolk. On low, mix in flour and salt. Mix in chopped pecans. Chill dough for one hour.

Using a 1 inch scoop, drop on wax paper lined cookie sheets 3 inches apart. Place a pecan half on top. Bake for 12-14 minutes, rotating sheets halfway through. Cool completely.

Double-Dipped Chocolate Peanut Butter Cookies

1 ¼ cup all purpose flour
½ tsp. baking powder
½ tsp. baking soda
½ tsp. salt
½ cup sugar
½ cup brown sugar
½ cup peanut butter
1 egg
1 tsp. vanilla
1½ cup semisweet chocolate chips
3 tsp. shortening, divided
1 ½ cup milk chocolate chips

Makes 2 dozen 3 inch cookies.

Preheat oven to 350 degrees. Combine flour, baking powder, baking soda and salt in a small bowl. Beat 1 ½ tsp. butter, sugar, and brown sugar in a large bowl with an electric mixer. Beat in peanut butter, egg and vanilla. Add the flour mixture, blending well.
Roll heaping tablespoons of dough into 1 ½ inch balls. Place 2 inches apart on an ungreased cookie sheet. (If too soft to roll, chill for 30 minutes.) Use fork dipped in sugar, to flatten cookies in criss cross manner. Bake 12 minutes. Let stand on sheet for 2 minutes. Remove and cool completely. Melt both chocolates and 1 ½ tsp. butter. Dip cookies. Let stand until set.

Peanut Clusters

From Ann Perlman's "The Christmas Cookie Club"

1 tsp. vegetable oil
4 oz. semisweet chocolate
4 oz. milk chocolate
2 cups peanuts, chopped
Note: can also use pecans, almonds or cashews

In double boiler, place oil first, then melt chocolate. Stir in nuts.

Spoon by rounded teaspoons unto wax paper. Cool.

Chez Diana

Peanut Butter Oatmeal Cookies

Peanut Butter Oatmeal Cookies Recipe at Cooking.com

Ingredients

3 egg whites
1 cup packed brown sugar
1 cup reduced-fat peanut butter
½ cup unsweetened applesauce
¼ cup honey
2 teaspoons vanilla extract
3 cups quick-cooking oats
1 cup all-purpose flour
1 cup nonfat dry milk powder
2 teaspoons baking soda

Directions

In a mixing bowl, beat egg whites and brown sugar. Beat in peanut butter, applesauce, honey and vanilla. Combine the oats, flour, milk powder and baking soda; gradually add to peanut butter mixture, beating until combined. Drop by tablespoonfuls 2 in. apart onto baking sheets coated with nonstick cooking spray. Bake at 350 degrees F for 8-10 minutes or until golden brown. Remove to wire racks to cool.

Yield: 6 Dozen

Snickerdoodles

My mother's recipe
She credits Betty Crocker
Makes 5 dozen 2 inch cookies

1 cup shortening
  (I use unsalted butter)
1 ½ cup sugar
2 eggs
2 ¾ cup flour
2 tsp. cream of tartar
1 tsp. baking soda
¼ tsp. salt
For dipping: 4 Tbsp. sugar & 4 tsp.
  cinnamon
Or 4 Tbsp. colored sugar

Mix shortening, sugar, and eggs with electric mixer. Stir in the dry ingredients. Chill dough in refrigerator. Roll into balls the size of walnuts. Roll balls into dipping sugar. Place 2 inches apart on ungreased baking sheet. Bake at 400 degrees for 8-10 minutes. Cool on wire racks. Store in saran wrap lined aluminum tins. A Christmas favorite in my family for generations.

Chez Diana

Aunt Faye's Toll House Cookies

Preheat oven to 375 degrees

Ingredients

1 cup plus 1 Tbsp. sifted flour
1 ½ tsp. baking soda
½ cup shortening
6 Tbsp. granulated sugar
½ cup chopped walnuts
6 oz. semisweet chocolate chips
6 Tbsp. brown sugar
1 tsp. hot water
1 egg, beaten
¾ tsp. vanilla

Directions

In electric mixer, cream shortening, add sugar and brown sugar. Beat well and add egg. Add hot water, sifted flour, and baking soda and mix well. Add nuts, chocolate bits and vanilla. Drop by teaspoonful on lightly greased cookie sheets. Bake 10 minutes at 375 degrees. Cool on wire racks.

Peanut Butter Balls

Preheat oven to 300 degrees

Ingredients

1 cup peanut butter
1 egg
1 cup sugar
1 tsp. vanilla

Directions

Combine all ingredients and stir until well blended. Form into 1 inch balls. Bake on ungreased cookie sheets in a preheated 300 degree oven for 15 to 20 minutes or until lightly browned.

Makes 2 ½ dozen cookies.

Chez Diana

Paula's Luau Coconut Pie

Recipe courtesy Paula Deen

4 tablespoons (½ stick) butter, melted
2 eggs, beaten
1 tablespoon all-purpose flour (recommended: Mochinko flour)
¾ cup sugar
1 (3 ½-ounce) can shredded sweetened coconut (about 1 cup)
1 cup coconut milk
1 (9-inch) unbaked pie shell

Preheat oven to 350 degrees F. In a large bowl, combine melted butter, eggs, flour, sugar, coconut, and milk. Pour into pie shell. Bake until firm, about 45 to 60 minutes.

Pineapple Blueberry Crunch Cake

Paula Deen's Best Dishes
Servings: 8 servings
Prep Time: 10 min; Cook Time: 45 min

Ingredients

¾ cup butter, plus more for dish
1 (20-ounce) can crushed pineapple, in juice
1 (20-ounce) can blueberry pie filling
1 (18.25-ounce) box yellow cake mix
1 cup chopped pecans

Directions

Preheat oven to 350 degrees F. Butter a 13 by 9-inch casserole dish.

Melt ¾ cup butter in saucepan over low heat.

Pour the pineapple with juice into the casserole dish and evenly spread blueberry pie filling on top. Cover with dry yellow cake mix and top with pecans. Drizzle with melted butter and bake for 35 to 45 minutes.

Chez Diana

Strawberry-Lemon Dessert

1986 Southern Living Cookbook

1 3-oz. package ladyfingers, split
1 14-oz. can sweetened
  condensed milk
1 Tbsp. grated lemon rind
$^1/_3$ cup lemon juice
1 pint whipping cream, whipped
  & divided
6-8 strawberries

Serves 6-8

Line bottom and sides of 2 ½ quart soufflé or flat sided dish with ladyfingers (rounded side down). Set aside. Combine sweetened condensed milk, lemon juice and lemon rind in medium bowl with hand electric mixer. Add $^2/_3$ of whipped cream and mix. Spread lemon mixture over ladyfingers. Spread remaining whipped cream on top. Cover and chill 3-4 hours. Place strawberries on top to serve.

Nut Goodies Candy – Easy

Recipe courtesy of Ericka Hall, Hayward, CA
Makes about 4 dozen.
(From ANG Newspapers Annual Cookie/Candy contest; Daily Review, Dec 2006)

12 ounces chocolate chips
12 ounces butterscotch chips
1 ounce unsweetened baking
  chocolate
2 cups creamy peanut butter
12 ounces Spanish peanuts

Filling:
2 sticks butter
½ cup evaporated milk
¼ cup dry vanilla pudding mix
  (not instant)
1 teaspoon maple flavoring
2 pounds powdered sugar

Melt chocolate chips, butterscotch chips, baking chocolate and peanut butter together. Pour half the mixture into a buttered 12-by-16-inch baking pan. Place in the freezer to set. Keep the remaining mixture in the pan. In a separate pan, combine the butter, evaporated milk and pudding mix and bring to a boil, stirring constantly. Boil for 1 minute, then remove from the heat. Add maple flavoring and stir in the powdered sugar. Spread over the cooled chocolate mixture in the baking pan and return to the freezer. Rewarm the remaining chocolate mixture on the stove and stir in the Spanish peanuts. Spread over the chilled filling and return to the freezer once again until all three layers have hardened. Remove chilled candy from freezer and let stand for 10 to 15 minutes before cutting into 1-inch squares. Store in a covered container in the freezer or refrigerator.

Gina's Banana Cupcakes

Recipe courtesy The Neelys
Yield: 12 cupcakes
Times: Preparation -15 min; Cook-20 min; Total-35 min

Ingredients

Batter:

1 cup all-purpose flour
½ teaspoon baking powder
½ teaspoon baking soda
¼ teaspoon salt
1 stick butter, softened
½ cup sugar
¼ cup sour cream
1 ½ teaspoons vanilla extract
2 large eggs
2 large ripe bananas, peeled, and mashed
½ cup chopped walnuts, (reserve some for garnish)

Molasses Frosting: (I halve this)

2 tablespoons whole milk
1 ½ teaspoons vanilla extract
2 tablespoons butter, softened
4 ounces cream cheese, softened
2 tablespoons molasses
2 to 3 cups powdered sugar
Preheat the oven to 350 degrees F.

Directions

Batter: Line 1 (12-cup) muffin pan with paper cupcake liners. In a medium bowl, combine the flour, baking powder, baking soda, and salt. Set aside. In a large bowl, add the butter and the sugar. Beat with a hand-held mixer until combined. Add the sour cream and the vanilla extract. Slowly beat in the eggs, 1 at a time. Incorporate the dry mixture and wet mixtures together until thoroughly combined. Add the bananas and walnuts, being careful not to over mix. Using an ice cream scoop, fill each cupcake liner ¾ way full. Bake in the preheated oven until the tops turn golden-brown and when a toothpick, inserted in the middle of the cupcake, comes out clean, about 20 minutes. Remove the cupcakes from the oven to a wire rack and let cool before frosting.

Frosting:

In a large bowl, add the butter and cream cheese. Beat together until incorporated. Add the molasses and mix well. Stir in the vanilla extract, milk and powdered sugar.

Heavily frost the cupcakes and garnish with reserved chopped walnuts.

Hot Fudge Pudding Cake

If you have cold, brewed coffee on hand, it can be used in place of the instant coffee and water, but make sure it isn't too strong (use 1 cup of cold coffee mixed with ½ cup of water.) Serve the cake warm with vanilla or coffee ice cream. Leftovers can be reheated, covered with plastic wrap, in a microwave oven.

2 teaspoons instant coffee (or 1 c. brewed coffee)
1 ½ cups water (or if using brewed coffee, ½ cup water)
²/₃ cup Dutch-processed cocoa powder (2 ½ ounces), divided
¹/₃ cup brown sugar (packed, 1 ¾ ounces)
1 cup granulated sugar (7 ounces)
6 tablespoons unsalted butter
2 ounces semisweet chocolate or bittersweet chocolate, chopped
¾ cup unbleached all-purpose flour (3 ¾ ounces)
2 teaspoons baking powder
1 tablespoon vanilla extract
¹/₃ cup whole milk
¼ teaspoon table salt
1 large egg yolk

1. Adjust oven rack to lower-middle position and heat oven to 325 degrees. Lightly spray 8-inch square glass or ceramic baking dish with nonstick cooking spray. Stir instant coffee into water; set aside to dissolve (or 1 cup brewed coffee with ½ cup water, if using).

   Stir together ¹/₃ cup cocoa, brown sugar, and ¹/₃ cup granulated sugar in small bowl, breaking up large clumps with fingers; set aside.

   Melt butter, remaining ¹/₃ cup cocoa, and chocolate in small bowl in microwave; whisk until smooth and set aside to cool slightly.

   Whisk flour and baking powder in small bowl to combine; set aside. Whisk remaining ²/₃ cup sugar, vanilla, milk, and salt in medium bowl until combined; whisk in yolk.

   Add chocolate mixture and whisk to combine. Add flour mixture and whisk until batter is evenly moistened.

2. To assemble, pour batter into prepared baking dish and spread evenly to sides and corners. Sprinkle cocoa/sugar mixture evenly over batter (cocoa mixture should cover entire surface of batter); pour coffee mixture gently over cocoa mixture. Bake until cake is puffed and bubbling and just beginning to pull away from sides of baking dish, about 45 minutes. (Do not overbake.) Cool cake in dish on wire rack about 25 minutes before serving.

Chez Diana

Bacardi Rum Cake

Cake

1 cup chopped pecans
1 18-½ oz. package of yellow cake
  mix
1 3-¾ oz. package instant vanilla
  pudding
4 eggs
½ cup water
½ cup Bacardi rum
½ cup vegetable oil

Grease and flour a Bundt pan.
Sprinkle pecans in bottom of the
pan. Mix all the cake ingredients
in an electric mixer. Pour batter
over pecans in Bundt pan. Bake
one hour at 325 degrees. Cool.
Remove to serving dish. Prick top
with fork. Drizzle glaze over top
and sides.

Glaze

¼ lb. butter
¼ cup water
1 cup sugar
½ cup rum
Melt butter in small sauce pan.
Stir in water and sugar. Boil for
5 minutes, stirring constantly.
Remove from heat. Stir in the rum.

Optional – serve decorated with
maraschino cherries and/or
whipped cream.

Chez Diana

Sunny Banana Pie

Bananas and coconut in a yummy pie.

Ingredients
1 9-inch graham cracker crust
2 bananas
1 8-oz. package cream cheese, softened
2 cups milk
1 3 ¼ oz. package instant vanilla pudding
Toasted coconut

Directions
Slice bananas into bottom and sides of pie crust. Gradually add ½ cup milk into cream cheese mix until well blended. Add pudding mix and remaining milk and beat slowly for one minute. Pour into the crust over the sliced bananas. Garnish with toasted coconut. Chill and serve.

Hawaiian Delight Cake

Ingredients
3 cups all purpose flour
1 tsp. baking soda
1 tsp. cinnamon
2 cups sugar
1 tsp. salt
3 eggs
1 ½ cup vegetable oil
1 ½ tsp. vanilla
2 sliced bananas
1 can (8-oz.) crushed pineapples, undrained
Confectioner's sugar

Directions
Mix together flour, baking soda, cinnamon, sugar and salt. Add eggs and oil and vanilla to dry ingredients. Add bananas and pineapples with juice. Beat on slow speed of electric mixer until just well combined. Do not overbeat. Pour into greased bundt pan and bake at 350 degrees for 1 hour and 20 minutes. Cool in pan on rack. Turn out onto serving plate. Dust with Confectioner's sugar or use optional glaze below. Cake will remain for several days if wrapped and refrigerated.

Optional topping – Cream together until smooth 1 stick softened butter, 1 ½ cup Confectioner's sugar, 8 oz. package softened cream cheese, and 2 tsp. vanilla.

Pie Crust

Use a food processor.

Ingredients

1 cup flour
$^1/_3$ cup butter (frozen, cut in 1 inch
 pieces)
¼ tsp. salt (do not omit)
3 Tbsp. cold water

Directions

Process flour, salt and butter (5 pulses). Pour the water through the spout. Process until it forms a ball. Remove from processor and roll out. Place in a 9 inch pie pan. Bake, if necessary, 8-10 minutes at 475 degrees.

Double this to make a covered pie. Or double to make 2 pie crusts.

Banana Cream Pie

My mother's recipe.

For the pie:
1 cup sugar
$^1/_3$ cup corn starch
3 egg yolks
½ tsp. salt
2 ¼ cup milk
2 tsp. butter, melted

Scald milk. Mix sugar, corn starch, egg yolks and salt. Add to scalded milk and stir until thick. Pour into baked pie crust.

For meringue:
3 egg whites
6 Tbsp. sugar

Beat egg whites and sugar until stiff peaks form. Spoon on top of pie. Bake for 10 minutes at 375 degrees.

Old Fashioned Banana Pudding

6 tbsp. flour
1 c. sugar
2 ½ c. milk
2 or 3 egg yolks, can use whole egg but separate & beat separately
Vanilla flavoring
½ stick butter
Dash of salt

Mix flour and sugar first to prevent lumping. Mix all ingredients except vanilla. Microwave on high using whisk to stir every 2 minutes until desired thickness is achieved. Add vanilla and pour over bananas and wafers.

Chez Diana

Key Lime Pie

Source: Burt Wolf's Origins, Yukon
Active Time: 20 Minutes | Total Time: 1 Hour 10 Minutes
Yield: Makes 8 servings

Ingredients

For the Crust:
$^1/_3$ cup plus 1 teaspoon melted margarine
1 ½ cups crushed graham crackers
¼ cup granulated sugar

For the Filling:
Two 14-ounce cans sweetened condensed milk
5 large egg yolks
Grated zest of 1 lime
1 cup fresh lime juice

For The Crust:
Preheat the oven to 350 degrees F.

Directions

Coat the inside of a 9-inch-diameter deep-dish pie dish with 1 teaspoon of the melted margarine.

In a mixing bowl, combine the crushed graham crackers, sugar, and $^1/_3$ cup of melted margarine. When the ingredients are fully combined, use the mixture to line the bottom and sides of the pie dish. Place the pie dish into the preheated oven and bake for 10 minutes.

For The Filling:
While the crust is baking, in a mixing bowl, make the filling by whisking together all the ingredients.

When the crust is baked, remove it from the oven and pour in the filling. Return the filled pie crust to the oven and bake for 10 minutes more. Let cool to room temperature.

Chez Diana

Bread Pudding with Class
Chocolate-Walnut Bread Pudding

By Bet Merriman, Parade Food Editor

No one would ever guess that this suavely elegant dessert was any relation to its county cousin – old fashioned bread pudding! Beneath a crunchy topping enhanced with a scattering of walnuts is a velvet-smooth chocolate custard – a delectable texture contrast. Garnish with a coronet of whipped cream.

Ingredients

1 package (6 oz.) semisweet chocolate chips
3 cups milk, divided
½ tsp. salt
3 eggs, slightly beaten
¾ cup sugar
1 tsp. vanilla
¾ tsp. cinnamon
8 slices of dry bread
½ cup walnuts

Directions

Melt chocolate chips in 1 cup milk over medium heat (I use microwave.) Stir in remaining 2 cups of milk; reserve.

Combine the remaining ingredients except bread and water. Stir into reserved milk mixture.

Trim crusts from bread; cut into ½ inch cubes.

Pour bread cubes into a 1 ½ quart casserole. Pour milk-egg mixture over bread cubes, making sure that all cubes are saturated.

Scatter walnuts over the surface.

Set casserole in a pan of warm water. Bake at 350 degrees for 1 hour to 1 hour and 15 minutes. Pudding is done when a knife inserted in the center comes out clean.

When cool, garnish with a frill of whipped cream, if desired.

Glazed Pound Cake

From Southern Living 1989 Annual Recipes Cookbook

Ingredients

1 cup butter or margarine, softened
¼ cup shortening
3 cups sugar
5 eggs
3 cups all purpose flour
½ tsp. baking powder
½ tsp. salt
1 cup milk
1 tsp. rum extract
1 tsp. coconut extract
1 cup Confectioner's sugar
½ cup water
1 tsp. almond extract

Cream butter, shortening and sugar, beating well at medium speed of electric mixer. Add eggs, one at a time, beating well after each addition. Combine flour, baking powder, and salt; add to creamed mixture alternately with milk, beginning and ending with the flour mixture. Mix until just blended after each addition. Stir in rum and coconut extracts. Pour batter into a greased pan. Bake at 325 degrees for 1 ½ hour. Cool in pan for 10 minutes, remove from pan and cook completely. Combine powdered sugar, water and almond extract in a small pan. Boil and cook until sugar is dissolved. Pour glaze slowly over cooled cake.

My family has a long tradition of fondues. This cake, along with fruit, is a wonderful dipper for chocolate or dessert fondues.

Molten Chocolate Cakes with Irish Cream

Prep time: 10 minutes, Cook time: 10 to 12 minutes

½ cup butter
4 oz. bittersweet chocolate
2 large eggs
¼ cup sugar
1 tbsp. Irish cream liqueur
1 tbsp. flour
8 tbsp. Irish cream liqueur, divided
(optional garnish)

Makes 4 servings.

Preheat oven to 450°F and lightly butter four (4-oz.) ramekins. Place butter and chocolate in a medium glass bowl; microwave on HIGH for about 2 minutes, stirring twice, until butter and chocolate are melted. Add eggs, sugar and liqueur; beat with electric mixer until foamy. Beat in flour just until combined. Pour equal amounts of batter into ramekins; bake for 8 to 10 minutes or until set around the edges and soft in the middle. Let stand for 5 minutes, then invert onto 4 small plates. Pour 2 tbsp. Irish cream liqueur around the edge of each, if you like.

Chez Diana

Tiramisu

From John's Aunt Irene Farina

Ingredients

1 package Italian lady fingers
Rum
16 oz. tub of mascarpone
1 ½ cup sugar
4 eggs
3 T. cocoa or instant coffee powder
Amaretti Cookies (Vicenzi
  Amaretto d'Italia – same ones as
  in red square cans)

Directions

In a 9 X 13 inch pan lay out lady fingers. Sprinkle well with rum (till wet but not soaked). With mixer beat the eggs with the sugar until foamy. Add the mascarpone and cocoa or instant coffee and mix well. Pour the mascarpone over the rum soaked lady fingers. Crush the amaretti cookies and sprinkle over the mascarpone. Sprinkle again with rum. Sprinkle the top with cocoa. Cover tightly with saran wrap and freeze at least overnight.

Cut to serve in squares. Store in freezer.

Tiramisu

From Rita Sala, John's cousin

Ingredients

5 eggs separated
1.1 lbs ricotta (or ½ ricotta & ½
  mascarpone)
¼ cup powdered sugar
2 T. expresso (made)
Ladyfingers/Biscotti (Pavesini)
Amaretti Cookies or Cocoa

Mix 5 egg yolks with powdered sugar. Add coffee and mix. Add cheese and mix.

Whip egg whites until stiff peaks. Add egg whites to cheese mixture 2 spoonfuls at a time (folding in). Line a 9 X 12 dish with ladyfingers dipped/soaked in almond liquor. Layer ½ cheese mixture then another layer of soaked ladyfingers then remaining cheese mixture. On top sprinkle ground amarettis soaked with almond liquor and dust with cocoa. Cover with plastic wrap and freeze for at least one day. Keep leftovers frozen or refrigerated.

Chez Diana

Pecan Cheesecake

From Southern Living 1985 Annual Recipes Cookbook

Ingredients

For Crust:

1 ½ cups graham cracker crumbs
2 tablespoons sugar
¼ cup plus 2 Tbsp. butter, melted

Combine ingredients, mixing well. Press mixture into bottom of a 10-inch springform pan. Chill.

For Cheesecake:

5 (8-oz.) packages cream cheese, softened
1 ²/₃ cups packed light brown sugar
5 eggs
1 tsp. vanilla
1 cup chopped pecans

Directions

Beat cream cheese with electric mixer until light and fluffy; gradually add brown sugar, mixing well. Add eggs, one at a time, beating well after each addition. Stir in vanilla and 1 cup of pecans. Spoon into prepared springform pan. Bake at 325 degrees for one hour. Turn off oven; allow cheesecake to cool in the oven for 10 minutes. Remove and let cool to room temperature. Then refrigerate for 8 hours.

Remove sides of springform pan. Serve.

Yield – 12 servings

Chez Diana

Chez Diana

Recipe Index

Chez Diana

Chez Diana

Chapter Index

Chez Diana

Chez Diana

Chez Diana